John C. Baker

Non-Proliferation Incentives for Russia and Ukraine

Routledge
Taylor & Francis Group

LONDON AND NEW YORK

Adelphi Paper **309**

First published May 1997 by **Oxford University Press** for
The International Institute for Strategic Studies
23 Tavistock Street, London WC2E 7NQ

This reprint published by Routledge
2 Park Square, Milton Park, Abingdon, Oxon, OX14 4RN
For the International Institute for Strategic Studies
Arundel House, 13-15 Arundel Street, Temple Place, London, WC2R 3DX
www.iiss.org

Simultaneously published in the USA and Canada
By Routledge
711 Third Avenue, New York, NY 10017

Routledge is an imprint of the Taylor & Francis Group, an informa business

© The International Institute for Strategic Studies 1997

British Library Cataloguing in Publication Data
Data available

Library of Congress Cataloguing in Publication Data

ISBN 0-19-829371-2
ISSN 0567-932X

contents

tables

glossary

AEOI	Atomic Energy Organisation of Iran
CTR	Cooperative Threat Reduction programme
EBRD	European Bank for Reconstruction and Development
ELV	Expendable launch vehicle
ESA	European Space Agency
EU	European Union
EURATOM	European Atomic Energy Community
G-7	Group of Seven industrialised nations
HEU	Highly enriched uranium
IAEA	International Atomic Energy Agency
ICBM	Intercontinental ballistic missile
INF	Intermediate-range Nuclear Forces
ISRO	Indian Space Research Organisation
KEDO	Korean Peninsula Energy Development Organisation
LEU	Low enriched uranium
LWR	Light-water reactor
MAPI	Ministry of Atomic Power and Energy (Soviet Union)
MINATOM	Ministry of Atomic Energy (Russia)
MIRV	Multiple independently targetable re-entry vehicle
MOU	Memorandum of Understanding
MOX	Mixed-oxide fuel

MPC&A .... Materials protection, control and accounting
MTCR .... Missile Technology Control Regime
NASA .... National Aeronautics and Space
                                              Administration (US)
NGOS .... Non-governmental organisations
NPT .... Nuclear Non-Proliferation Treaty
NSG .... Nuclear Suppliers Group
PACATOM .... Pacific Atomic Energy Community
SLBMS .... Submarine-launched ballistic missiles
SLV .... Space-launch vehicle
START .... Strategic Arms Reduction Treaty
USEC .... United States Enrichment Corporation
WMD .... Weapons of mass destruction

introduction

With the demise of the Soviet Union in 1991, a new group of military technology providers has emerged. These are companies which used to operate strictly within the Soviet system and which are now encouraged to compete globally. Such enterprises pose a major challenge to non-proliferation regimes. They are often willing to sell sensitive dual-use technologies, material or expertise in order to break into highly competitive international markets. As a result of these sales, potential proliferators may be able to develop weapons of mass destruction (WMD) or missile-delivery systems. These transactions thus need to be subject to stricter controls. To offset the potential proliferation risks, the international community will need to consider new strategies to influence the businesses that are the source of the problem.

The former Soviet defence and nuclear industries pose special challenges because they combine several worrisome characteristics. First, they are potentially attractive sources of sophisticated and proven military technologies for foreign proliferators. Second, their managers need the revenues that come from aggressively exporting technology and services. Third, the usual policy-making checks on such sensitive exports have been eroded by fragmented bureaucratic controls. Political leaders are reluctant to curtail the prospects for these firms to earn hard currency or promote vital trade relations. Thus, the risk exists that such enterprises will sell sensitive technologies or know-how without regard to whether these transfers help proliferators to acquire advanced weapon systems.

Many disputes among leading Western suppliers over the proliferation risks of a particular technology-transfer decision have been settled ultimately at the heads-of-state level, mainly on the basis of larger political considerations. By contrast, the desperate economic situation of many former Soviet republics only increases their determination to earn foreign revenues, particularly hard currency. Hence, economic considerations exercise an unprecedented influence over the export decisions of struggling governments and their cash-starved enterprises. This situation requires the international community to consider a new combination of incentives and sanctions to counter the potential risks posed by these technology providers.

The primary purpose of this paper is to analyse the role of international incentives as part of a non-proliferation strategy. The aim must be to encourage former Soviet defence enterprises to adopt more responsible export policies for sensitive dual-use technologies and expertise, particularly in transactions with foreign countries and businesses whose commitments to non-proliferation are questionable or unknown. Special attention is given to the potential benefits of using incentives (e.g., political, economic and technological) to deal with emerging technology providers. The Cold War's end has created novel opportunities to influence the former Soviet republics on security issues. International efforts to encourage Ukraine's denuclearisation commitment and the positive resolution of the United States–Russia dispute over Moscow's plans to sell rocket-engine technology to India's space agency are good illustrations. Although the threat of sanctions continues to be a useful and proven instrument, under the right conditions political and economic incentives may offer a potentially lower-cost and more productive means for encouraging cooperation. Nonetheless, the implicit threat of economic sanctions triggered by unacceptable export behaviour remains an important source of political leverage.

the implicit threat of economic sanctions remains an important source of leverage

This study argues in favour of considering ambitious strategies that not only aim to influence a country's *behaviour* in specific export cases, but also seek long-term changes in the *attitudes* of its industrial and political élite. In the near term, international incentives could encourage greater self-restraint in the export policies of former Soviet defence and nuclear industries. The target audience for these incentives must be the top managers of key dual-use technology enterprises who are determined to keep their workforces and organisations intact, even if severely downsized compared to the Soviet era. These managers are most influenced by economic incentives (or disincentives) that affect their access to new commercial markets, their chances of being involved in major international scientific and technical projects, and opportunities for joint ventures with successful foreign firms.

The ultimate aim is to encourage enterprises in the former Soviet republics to exercise *leadership by example*, and guide their counterparts in other dual-use technology enterprises. This requires the international community to help firms demonstrating an unambiguous commitment to the non-proliferation of sensitive dual-use technologies with significantly better opportunities to attract foreign funds and participate in multinational projects.

Chapter 1 examines the political and economic developments that complicate national efforts to exert tight control over these enterprises and their export activities. It also explores new opportunities for using incentives to affect the export policies of the former Soviet defence industries. Subsequent chapters assess the potential role for incentives in dealing with two prominent technology providers: Ukraine's space-launch industry; and Russia's nuclear industry.

This paper concludes with some observations on the practical political and economic challenges associated with using international incentives to influence both the export behaviour and non-proliferation attitudes of emerging technology providers. These challenges include changing the attitudes of industry managers and government leaders towards non-proliferation, particularly when using international incentives is likely to be constrained by competing policy objectives and unanticipated domestic political developments.

Proliferation Risks: Formulating A New Strategy

The emergence of new technology suppliers in industrialising countries has received much attention.[1] Although concern about the risks posed by suppliers is a familiar theme, the former Soviet defence and nuclear enterprises offer a somewhat distinct challenge to existing non-proliferation regimes. Exports from these industries are potential problems because they could provide proliferating nations with an attractive source of proven, dual-use technologies. At the same time, the domestic economic and social conditions within the former Soviet republics place unprecedented pressure on their policy-makers and industry managers.

Non-proliferation experts are rightly concerned that these enterprises could engage in questionable exports of dual-use technology. In developing a strategy for dealing with this challenge, international supporters of a robust non-proliferation regime have a wide array of instruments at their disposal that can help diminish the potential risks created by these emerging technology providers. Along with more traditional tools, such as export controls and the threat of sanctions for irresponsible export behaviour, the international community can make greater use of an incentive strategy to influence former Soviet defence and nuclear enterprises in the short term. Equally important, long-term incentives can be targeted at managers and key subgroups to emphasise the importance of non-proliferation considerations in making export decisions. Such incentives seek to give industrial élites a substantial organisational inducement to undertake responsible export policies.

Imperatives Driving Technology Providers

The most significant factor shaping the external activities of the former Soviet dual-use technology industries is a compelling requirement for foreign revenues, particularly hard currency. This economic imperative stems from the need to compensate for the substantial loss of internal revenue sources that the industries enjoyed when they were major elements of the Soviet Union's military-industrial complex. Over the past decade, these industries have steadily lost their privileged position within this economic and social system. In a highly centralised economy, they had priority access to skilled personnel, investment, suppliers and the distribution of their products. But the break-up of the Soviet Union sharply curtailed government orders and reduced revenues to a fraction of their previous level.[2] By exporting dual-use technologies, specialised know-how and technical services, these ailing industries are trying to sustain their current operations, stave off further job losses and generate investment funds for future programmes.

Efforts to convert to purely commercial activities are hampered by several factors – the geographical isolation of formerly closed cities, insufficient development of the commercial technology sector compared with the military sector, cultural resistance to systemic changes, severely limited funds for retraining highly specialised defence workers and the sheer magnitude of the problem. Given the uncertain prospects for internal defence conversion programmes and Western efforts to offer a better alternative – at least in the short term – for adjusting to the post-Cold War economic environment, advanced technology industries want to break into foreign markets. As a result, many managers view dual-use technology exports as a less painful alternative to major restructuring.[3]

the most significant factor is a compelling need for foreign revenues

The social character of the technology businesses in the former Soviet republics reinforces the economic constraints facing decision-makers. The Soviet Union's defence and nuclear enterprises provided a broad range of social services, such as housing, health care and cultural activities for employees and their families, which in Western countries would be the responsibility of individuals or local governments.[4] Substantially reduced revenues for these enterprises now mean unprecedented hardships for the larger communities of family members and support personnel who also depended on them. The fact that most of these industries are densely concentrated in certain regions and cities, or even in relatively isolated industrial or scientific centres, only increases the pressure on managers to take whatever steps are necessary to preserve the core workforce and sustain its dependent population.[5]

At the same time, the changed political and economic circumstances also create opportunities and temptations for individuals and groups at all levels to seek personal financial gain by facilitating the transfer of sensitive technologies and expertise to foreign customers. The executives who run these enterprises have their own professional and personal stakes in using exports to generate needed resources. Their success in earning foreign revenue could be vital to maintaining their relatively privileged position. But the motive behind the strong push for dual-use technology exports is unambiguous: economic survival in a time of severely constrained sources of domestic funding.

Ambivalence about Non-Proliferation

The technology firms in the former Soviet republics operate in an environment where national policy-making processes tend to be ambivalent about non-proliferation concerns. The industries as a whole are politically influential actors or at least enjoy the support of powerful national leaders. They are often key elements in the economic development plans of the central government. In some cases, the enterprises still enjoy a certain degree of national prestige and importance as torch-bearers of the earlier Soviet military strength and international standing. Hence, the continuing survival of these firms is frequently portrayed by national government officials as crucial to maintaining the country's power base and revitalising its advanced technology sector.

Hard-currency flows generated by these firms add to their political clout within the national policy-making process of countries such as Russia and Ukraine. The proven or potential ability of the industries to attract foreign revenues places them in a domestic political situation that is difficult to challenge. National leaders either actively support these enterprises or are disinclined to interfere with their operations. This situation means that bureaucratic counterparts to these industries, such as the Ministry of Foreign Affairs or export-control organisations, find themselves in a relatively weak position to curtail, or even question, the export activities of these firms. In some cases, the bureaucrat scrutinising technology-export proposals for non-proliferation implications might not be aware of industry plans, or at least the critical details, until after the export decisions have been made.

Finally, pursuing consistent non-proliferation policies is complicated by coordination and implementation problems within the former Soviet republics. For many·of the new states, the policy-making process for dealing with technology-export issues is still evolving and their export-control systems are being developed almost from scratch. Of course, Russia faces a somewhat different problem. Unlike the other former Soviet states, Russia inherited a well-developed administrative structure for making decisions about technology exports. But Moscow now faces the daunting task of updating its administrative structures and reorienting its industrial organisations to new circumstances.[6]

Proliferation Risks

Although the weapons-proliferation problem is not wholly driven by technology suppliers, imprudent or inadvertent exports of sensitive technologies could greatly facilitate the global spread of WMD and their delivery systems. While purely indigenous efforts might suffice for some countries, other proliferating nations have significantly bolstered their acquisition of advanced weapon capabilities by importing dual-use technologies and drawing on foreign expertise. Timely imports of sensitive technologies can offer proliferating nations numerous benefits, including:

- reducing the length of time required to acquire WMD or a delivery system;
- diminishing the scientific risks of weapons acquisition, as well as helping to avoid major delays and dead-ends;
- reducing the financial burden of acquiring these weapons; and
- increasing the reliability and sophistication of the final weapon designs.

Proliferation of such technology can reduce the hurdles and costs facing importing countries. The spread of advanced weapon technologies can be promoted in several ways by:

- the deliberate export of sensitive dual-use technologies or know-how integral to manufacturing advanced weapon systems;
- the inadvertent transfer of information or sensitive items by enterprises that are not fully aware of their proliferation significance; and
- the transfer of sensitive dual-use technologies and commodities to unknown end-users.

In addition, the difficult economic and social conditions of the former Soviet defence industries encourages the unauthorised leakage of dual-use technologies and expertise by industry insiders or groups with illegal access to such items. Thus, the unrestrained activities of emerging technology providers could undermine non-proliferation regimes striving to make the acquisition of WMD and long-range missile systems a protracted, expensive and technically demanding process.

Instruments Supporting Non-Proliferation Regimes

With the end of the Cold War, the array of non-proliferation instruments available to the international community has significantly expanded to include more cooperative and incentive-based strategies. However, any effective use of incentives to influence the export policies of emerging technology providers must occur within a broader strategy, which is likely to include more traditional instruments such as the use of persuasion, diplomatic pressure and even economic sanctions.

Persuasion has often been sufficient to convince many countries to join or at least abide by the diverse treaties and understandings that constitute the international non-proliferation regime. In the nuclear area, these constraints on weapons-related technologies and materials are rooted in the Nuclear Non-Proliferation Treaty (NPT) and other agreements, such as the safeguard agreements associated with the International Atomic Energy Agency (IAEA). Acceptance of non-proliferation standards can also be reflected by membership in the various technology supplier control groups, including the Nuclear Suppliers Group (NSG), the Non-Proliferation Treaty Exporters (or Zangger Committee), the Missile Technology Control Regime (MTCR) and the Australia Group, which focuses on chemical precursors and related technical data.[7] Many countries join these institutions for a variety of reasons, including perceived security interests, a desire for international standing, encouragement by other countries or an expectation that not being a member will result in negative political or trade consequences. Unfortunately, persuasion itself is not always sufficient to encourage all countries to adhere to these agreements and practices. Even though most of the former Soviet republics are now parties to these pacts, some of their emerging technology providers have been accused of engaging in questionable export practices.

Diplomatic pressure has been applied in the past by one or several countries against another whose scientific enterprises apparently do not comply with the various non-proliferation agreements or understandings. As a relatively powerful country and a leading non-proliferation proponent, the us has frequently undertaken diplomatic *démarches* to alert allies and other countries to Washington's concern about the risks involved in specific transactions. Serious disagreements over a controversial transfer have often been resolved when the issue was raised and settled at top political levels on the basis of broader alliance concerns. In some specific cases, diplomatic and economic pressure appears to have been instrumental in discouraging international transactions that could have contributed to weapons proliferation. In the mid-1970s, for example, pressure was crucial in persuading Paris to suspend – by attaching conditions that Pakistan found unacceptable – an earlier French commitment to provide Pakistan with a reprocessing facility.[8] The effectiveness of using quiet pressure to encourage the former Soviet republics to adhere strictly to export controls on sensitive technology is uncertain, however, given the apparent unwillingness or inability of these political leaders to exercise control over their country's technology firms.

Sanctions are one of the most controversial elements of a nonproliferation strategy, particularly given the difficulties in assessing their ultimate effectiveness. Economic and political sanctions have often been threatened, and occasionally applied, with success. For example, in the mid-1970s the us and Canada pressured South Korea to drop its plans to purchase a nuclear reprocessing plant from France with the threat of political and economic sanctions.[9]

The US has also led an effort to apply sanctions against the so-called 'rogue' states (i.e., Iran, Iraq, Libya and North Korea) in an attempt to isolate them politically and deny them easy access to foreign investments and trading partners.

However, there are major constraints on attempts to make effective use of sanctions. They are much less likely to have the desired effect when competing foreign policy and economic interests are at stake. This is often the case when seeking to change the behaviour of a technology-exporting country that is also a leading military power or major trading partner of the country applying the sanctions. For example, the US has been reluctant to sustain strong sanctions against China despite evidence suggesting that it has transferred sensitive missile and nuclear-related technologies to Pakistan.[10] Furthermore, sanctions are most effective when based on multinational cooperation and usually least effective when unilaterally applied. In these circumstances, differences over applying sanctions can create major strains among allies and neighbouring states, as has been the case with the 1996 US Congress' Cuban Liberty and Democratic Solidarity (*Libertad*) Act (commonly known as the Helms–Burton Act) that threatens to penalise foreign individuals and companies doing business with Cuba.[11]

Despite the mixed record regarding the actual effectiveness of sanctions as a non-proliferation instrument, their ever-present threat probably gives some important credibility to international efforts. Even if sanctions have not always eliminated questionable export activities, they can raise the political saliency of the non-proliferation issue substantially and thereby increase the likelihood that the political leadership will give more consideration to external concerns.

New Opportunities for Incentives

Since the end of the Cold War, Western policies have given incentives a more prominent role in encouraging non-proliferation by Russia, Ukraine and other former Soviet republics. Recent experience encourages policy-makers to think of incentives as a complement to more traditional non-proliferation instruments. The potential utility of employing them has been demonstrated in several recent cases, including the US–Russian resolution of the *Glavkosmos* dispute and Ukraine's denuclearisation commitment.

Glavkosmos *and the Russian Space Programme*

In mid-1993, the US used political and economic incentives to resolve a festering dispute over the planned transfer of Russian space technology to India, which had triggered US trade sanctions against space enterprises in both countries. The controversial agreement committed *Glavkosmos*, the Russian industrial organisation responsible for arranging the deal, to sell cryogenic space booster engines to the Indian Space Research Organisation (ISRO). The ISRO wanted several Russian rocket engines as well as production technology for making its own engines. However, Washington objected to the transfer of rocket engines, claiming it was contrary to Moscow's pledge to abide by the MTCR. US officials believed that such technology would help India's military missile programme. On 11 May 1992, the US imposed trade sanctions against both *Glavkosmos* and the ISRO.[12]

As this issue began to strain broader US–Russian relations, the Clinton administration formulated an incentive strategy aimed at breaking the impasse. Washington obtained a commitment from Moscow to limit its transaction with India to the sale of rocket engines and not to transfer production technologies. In return, Russia was allowed to launch US commercial satellites, giving a significant prospect of earning hard currency. After 1993, the US and Russia began to pursue increasingly compatible non-proliferation and space-technology programmes. Moscow took steps to become a formal member of the MTCR in 1995. Having resolved the *Glavkosmos* controversy, Russia was eventually accepted as a full partner in the International Space Station programme, with the Russian Space Agency and its strong pro-Western orientation assuming a greater role in guiding Russia's space activities.

The *Glavkosmos* case highlights the emerging role of non-proliferation incentives in the aftermath of the Cold War. Although the sanctions applied against *Glavkosmos* and the ISRO indicated the seriousness of US concern over the proposed transaction, they were neither sufficient to halt the transaction nor to resolve the disagreement between Washington and Moscow. Instead, Moscow seems to have changed its plans mainly because of Washington's political and economic incentives. Russia needed to be convinced that its best prospects for gaining long-term access to Western space projects and markets was to adopt robust non-proliferation policies and to forego the short-term financial gains offered by questionable technology transfers.

Ukraine's Commitment to Denuclearisation

Western incentives also played a major role in facilitating Kiev's agreement to the January 1994 Trilateral Statement with Russia and the US. Under this agreement, Kiev was obliged to relinquish some 1,900 nuclear weapons remaining on Ukrainian territory by sending them to Russia for dismantlement.[13] In exchange, the US and Russia made a series of security assurances to Ukraine. Moscow also agreed to provide Ukraine with nuclear reactor fuel as compensation for the highly enriched uranium (HEU) in the warheads being returned to Russia. Washington pledged to give Kiev both financial and technical assistance to help eliminate nuclear forces and their related facilities located in Ukraine. The US also raised the prospect of space cooperation with Ukraine, including the possibility of eventually receiving commercial contracts for launching US satellites using Ukrainian space-launch vehicles (SLVs).

The joint statement, signed by Presidents Clinton, Yeltsin and Kravchuk, was instrumental in helping Kiev overcome its reservations about giving up all the nuclear weapons on its territory. This package – combining security assurances with economic and technical assistance – was a powerful incentive to Kiev, which was already questioning the wisdom of holding onto nuclear weapons given Ukraine's growing economic crisis.[14] The high-level agreement finally allowed the government of President Leonid Kuchma, who was elected in July 1994, to gain parliamentary support for the unconditional ratification of the first Strategic Arms Reduction Treaty (START) and Ukraine's accession to the NPT as a non-nuclear-weapon state.

Thus, Ukraine's decision to proceed with denuclearisation is a good example of the potential power of incentives to change a government's thinking. Despite some minor problems, Ukraine's commitment to this policy was successfully accomplished when the final shipment of nuclear weapons arrived in Russia in June 1996. The explicit economic and security incentives provided by Washington and Moscow were essential for overcoming Ukrainian ambivalence about relinquishing the nuclear arsenal it had inherited from the Soviet Union.

Other Cooperative Programmes

In addition to these specific cases where incentive strategies have been used to encourage non-proliferation, Western governments offer other assistance schemes to Belarus, Kazakstan, Russia and Ukraine for dismantling nuclear weapon systems and enhancing nuclear security and safety. Since 1991 most of the programmes for dismantling former Soviet nuclear weapons and eliminating excess nuclear delivery systems have been funded under the 1991 US Cooperative Threat Reduction Act (CTR) (a result of the US Congress' Nunn–Lugar legislation).[15] This funding has also resulted in the creation of international science and technology centres in Moscow and Kiev that support former Soviet weapon experts seeking re-employment in non-military work.[16] Other programmes provide assistance in upgrading the security arrangements at institutes and facilities that possess weapons-useable fissile materials. Some schemes are also dedicated to promoting defence conversion by encouraging US firms to work with former Soviet defence or nuclear enterprises. Each of these international assistance projects is intended to accomplish a specific task, but they also serve as incentives for overcoming bureaucratic resistance within the defence and nuclear establishments of the former Soviet states.

Formulating Incentive Strategies

An incentive strategy is defined here as a systematic approach to applying international incentives to influence both the behaviour and attitudes of decision-makers responsible for technology-exporting enterprises. It seeks to persuade industry managers, as well as political leaders, that their interests are better served over the long run by a strong commitment to the standards of a robust non-proliferation regime. The key elements of a such a plan include:

- determining the objective for non-proliferation incentive strategies;
- persuading the technology providers to adhere to the spirit of the non-proliferation regime;
- differentiating the target audiences for incentives; and
- encouraging government and private-sector partnerships to promote non-proliferation objectives.

Incentive Strategy Goals

Incentive strategies are best used to influence the export behaviour of dual-use industries or specific enterprises by making their actions more consistent with non-proliferation standards. In addition, incentives play a special role in encouraging changes in the attitudes of industrial and political élites regarding the importance of non-proliferation in making export plans and structuring the internal practices of their enterprises.

A long-term strategy should attempt to combine distinct objectives over varying time-scales. (See Table 1.) In the near term, the main goal is to influence the specific *behaviour* of companies and industries so they exhibit self-restraint in exporting sensitive dual-use technologies. In comparison, the mid-term focus should be on changing the general *attitudes* of top industry managers and their political leadership to give high priority to non-proliferation concerns. This is best achieved by convincing them that market-place success depends partly on whether desirable foreign partners and customers perceive a genuine commitment to robust non-proliferation policies. Finally, the main long-term objective is to encourage countries with much improved reputations for controlling sensitive technologies to set a positive example for other countries with technology exporting firms, as well as to assume a *leadership role* on non-proliferation issues when the opportunity arises.

Achieving these objectives will be difficult. The former Soviet defence and nuclear enterprises are torn between exploiting short term financial opportunities, even if they involve significant proliferation risks, and the desire to adhere to strong non-proliferation export policies either for policy reasons or simply to ensure good relations with Western firms.

'Letter versus Spirit'

The ambiguity surrounding what are acceptable exports only exacerbates the competing perspectives on dual-use technology exports. Confronted with strong economic and social pressures, the former Soviet enterprises are determined to pursue almost every opportunity for exporting dual-use technologies as a source of hard currency. Even under the best circumstances, the inclination of their managers is to follow only the *letter* of international or national

Table 1 *Essential Elements of a Non-Proliferation Incentive Strategy Relevant to Emerging Technology Providers*

	Near-term	**Mid-term**	**Long-term**
Main Objectives	Discourage irresponsible export behaviour	Change attitudes towards non-proliferation	Encourage countries to assume a leadership role
Key Target Audiences	Political leaders and industry managers	Industry managers, industry subgroups, political leaders and export control officials	Political leaders, industry managers, other executive and parliamentary actors (e.g., Ministry of Foreign Affairs)
Instruments for Encouraging Non-proliferation Policies	Foreign revenues, market access, technical assistance, threat of sanctions or the loss of ongoing or promised benefits	Foreign revenues, market access, joint ventures, scientific recognition, two-way technology transfers, and the threat of losing anticipated benefits	International recognition, and participation in prestigious projects

restrictions. Unless a national regulation or treaty obligation undertaken by their government specifically prohibits a technology transfer, then the enterprise managers feel free to pursue any available international business opportunity.

By contrast, supporters of a global non-proliferation policy contend that the treaty obligations only provide the necessary core for an effective regime and that additional forms of self-restraint are desirable. The US and its supporters thus focus more on the *spirit* of the agreement. They often insist on adopting additional measures that go beyond the requirements of official treaties and agreements to demonstrate a strong commitment to weapons non-proliferation. These might include restraints on certain types of technologies that should not be exported, or might involve internal measures, such as a rigorous national export-control system or enhanced customs monitoring and enforcement activities.

Non-proliferation incentive strategies can play an important role in striking a balance between these conflicting perspectives. In situations where a supplier is asked to refrain from technology transfer and business dealings that are not formally prohibited by its non-proliferation obligations, incentives can play a positive role by striking a balance between these disparate concepts. An incentive strategy is likely to identify specific political or economic incentives that offer more than adequate compensation to these governments and their dual-use technology enterprises. However, the short-term price for accepting these incentives will be to make demonstrable changes in export behaviour in ways that address the key concerns of the non-proliferation regime's strongest supporters. The longer-term objective of an effective incentive strategy is to improve the attitudes of the relevant government and industry élite by giving them a growing political and economic stake in pursuing export behaviour that is compatible with a robust non-proliferation regime.

Relating Incentives to Target Audiences

For a non-proliferation incentive strategy to be effective, the formulator must have a relatively clear idea of who the target audience (the individuals or groups to be influenced) is and whether that audience has sufficient authority to behave as desired. Specific political or economic incentives are unlikely to have a uniform influence on the groups that can affect the export behaviour of a particular firm. Although certain incentives must be tailored to the unique features and interests of the target audiences, there are generally five distinctive target groups.

In theory, *political leaders* have the national authority to restrain or change the export behaviour of businesses within their jurisdiction. In many cases, however, the leaders of the newly independent states might be unwilling to exercise power. Despite their statutory authority, they could opt to refrain from intervening in questionable decisions either because they condone the behaviour or because they are reluctant to impede efforts to generate hard currency. Even if these political leaders did have serious reservations about a firm's export policy, they might not have enough political power to succeed if they forced the issue. Nonetheless, any incentives offered by the international community must have some political appeal for these national decision-makers to succeed over the long term.

the inclination of managers is to follow only the letter of restrictions

The *top managers* of the former Soviet defence and nuclear enterprises should be considered the primary target audience for international incentives. They are most likely to be influenced by incentives that help them attain their key organisational goals, which include sustaining their day-to-day operations, preserving a core workforce, obtaining revenues for overdue re-capitalisation and expanding global market opportunities. In addition, these senior managers have personal interests in attracting international recognition and sustaining their privileged position at the enterprise.

Another important target audience is the key individuals and groups most likely to receive direct and indirect benefits from well-designed international incentives, such as lab-to-lab exchanges or industrial partnership programmes. These benefits can include a stable funding source, international recognition of their work and past accomplishments and opportunities for advancement in a particular technical field through information exchanges. Even though they lack the organisational power of top industry officials, these *industry subgroups* can still exert an important, indirect influence on the industry's behaviour by making officials consider the detrimental effects that controversial exports might have on specific cooperative programmes.

Other executive agencies and parliamentary actors are unlikely to have much bureaucratic or political influence over short-term export behaviour. Given the current political and economic situation among the former Soviet republics, such traditionally powerful actors as the Ministry of Foreign Affairs and the Ministry of Defence seem to exert relatively less influence over export policies than they did in Soviet times. Nonetheless, consideration should be given to how incentives may affect their interests within the policy-making process and whether they are likely to play a productive role in convincing industry officials to give more priority to non-proliferation concerns. These ministries are most likely to be concerned with the broader security implications of international dealings and with a desire to ensure that their country's interests are well represented.

Relevant *non-government players* include outside experts, the national media and public opinion. These actors are likely to exert very little influence on export behaviour under normal circumstances. However, international incentives directed at the other target audiences are unlikely to be sustainable over the long term if these non-governmental groups perceive that such incentives are generally detrimental to the country's overall national interests. Incentives featuring

top managers should be the primary target for incentives

highly focused technical programmes of interest to managers and industry subgroups probably need to be coupled with higher-profile symbolic gestures in order to reassure the public that specific technical incentives are resulting in national benefits. International incentives should also seek to strengthen domestic support in these countries for responsible non-proliferation policies.

Complementary Roles of the Government and the Private Sector

A key element in any incentive-driven non-proliferation strategy is the complementary roles that must be played by governments and the private sector to ensure success.[17] Given tight national budgets and the political difficulties of sustaining domestic support for long-term foreign-assistance programmes, the private sector's importance in providing economic opportunities for these former Soviet industries has considerably increased. Struggling dual-use enterprises are likely to find that a successful transition to the civilian economy is determined much more by market opportunities and competition than by foreign government assistance. Nonetheless, their progress in breaking into the commercial market is unlikely to be sustainable without at least indirect government involvement, particularly given the substantial role of outside governments in regulating the international market.

In many respects the foreign donor governments and the former Soviet republics continue to take the lead in formulating a non-proliferation relationship. The government that provides the technical or financial assistance usually plays a critical role in creating the conditions necessary for the recipient enterprises to receive the anticipated benefits, whether in financial and technical areas or simply opportunities to gain international recognition. Most importantly, the governments tend to regulate enterprise participation in the market through their export guidelines, international and quota agreements.

At the same time, for these anticipated benefits to be realised, the recipient government must also prove to contributing foreign governments that satisfactory progress is being made in adopting recommended non-proliferation measures. In addition, foreign commercial enterprises need some degree of assurance that any substantial investment of time and resources will not be wasted by bureaucratic inertia or even local corruption. Thus, active government involvement is probably necessary throughout the process to establish and convey clearly the non-proliferation behaviour that is expected from both the former Soviet defence enterprise and its foreign customers or partners. Outside governments are in the best position to discourage undesirable export behaviour by threatening to take appropriate countermeasures against the particular dual-use technology enterprise or its foreign partners.

Within the boundaries established by the governments, private-sector involvement is essential for two reasons. First, the international commercial market can help an emerging technology provider generate external sources of revenue to sustain its day-to-day operations while meeting its recapitalisation needs. Given the magnitude of the defence conversion problem associated with the former Soviet military-industrial complex, it is the private sector that possesses most of the capital and expertise that particular enterprises need to achieve some degree of economic revitalisation. Foreign commercial companies are better positioned to create joint ventures with emerging technology providers, invest much-needed capital in modernisation and purchase their products and services on a scale that makes a difference to the enterprise.

Second, outside firms can convince the managers of these enterprises of the practical importance of foregoing questionable transfers of technologies, materials and expertise. External private firms can probably convey with greater credibility the message that responsible non-proliferation is good business practice. Foreign firms are likely to play these important roles less out of altruism than because they see sound business reasons for becoming customers or partners of former Soviet companies. This has clearly occurred in the aerospace sector where several partnerships and subcontractor relationships have developed in the space-launch technology area.

Thus, non-proliferation incentive strategies require a relatively clear sense of which individuals and organisations are the focus of the effort. By carefully targeting the key decision-making audience and using incentives and disincentives directly related to their organisational interests, the international community can improve the chances of success. Success will also increase when foreign partners and customers make business cooperation conditional on former Soviet companies foregoing questionable export activities.

chapter 2

Redirecting Ukraine's Missile Industries

Although most of the former Soviet Union's ballistic-missile industrial base is located in Russia, numerous defence enterprises that once were integral to designing and producing strategic missiles and military space systems now belong to Ukraine. Among the largest and most prominent is the Southern Machine Building Plant Association, which is concentrated in the industrial city of Dnipropetrovsk. This conglomerate of missile research, design and production facilities, still known as *Yuzhnoye* or 'Southern', is reportedly the world's largest integrated rocket and satellite manufacturing enterprise.[1]

Like its Russian counterparts, *Yuzhnoye* faces daunting challenges in adapting to post-Cold War economic realities. Even though Kiev is strongly committed to preserving the core elements of the aerospace industry that it inherited from the Soviet Union, the long-term viability of *Yuzhnoye* and other aerospace enterprises largely depends on their ability to break into the international market for space technologies and launch services. If these enterprises are unable to find adequate civilian markets for their products, then they could become a source of dual-use technologies and expertise for countries trying to acquire long-range ballistic-missile systems. Ukraine's continuing economic difficulties, along with periodic reports of questionable dealings between Ukrainian enterprises and potential missile proliferators, pose a possible risk that the international community should address.

External efforts to encourage *Yuzhnoye's* management to give higher priority to non-proliferation concerns face major obstacles. These arise not only from the facility's almost desperate need for foreign revenues, but also from its legacy as a leading producer of powerful military missiles and its strong connections to Ukraine's political leaders. Under these complex conditions, how can the international community encourage a stronger non-proliferation commitment from Ukraine's leading aerospace enterprises? And more specifically, what role can international incentives and disincentives play in convincing both the political leadership in Kiev and *Yuzhnoye's* managers of the practical benefits of becoming a civilian space power that adheres to high non-proliferation standards?

Challenges for Enterprises in Transition

The Soviet Union's dissolution, coupled with the end of the East–West military competition, dramatically reduced the demand for traditional military and civilian space systems from the Soviet aerospace industry, including *Yuzhnoye's* products. Given their dire circumstances, many enterprise managers and even government officials now view exporting advanced technology products and expertise as the most promising means of developing new sources of revenues.

Problems facing Yuzhnoye

Yuzhnoye is attempting to retain some semblance of its previous industrial capabilities as it struggles with defence conversion. Although it once produced some of the world's most powerful missiles, *Yuzhnoye* now concentrates on manufacturing SLVs capable of placing either civilian or military satellites into orbit. It has substantial experience in designing and producing the *Zenit* and *Tsyklon* rockets, originally used to launch various types of Soviet payloads.

Severe cutbacks in government funding pose major problems for the firm as it tries to sustain its skilled workforce and maintain its specialised facilities. There are indications that the number of *Yuzhnoye's* employees has declined from about 54,000 to 45,000 at its production plant and from nearly 10,000 to 6,000 at its associated research and design organisation.[2] Although the large *Yuzhnoye* complex has also manufactured non-military items, an effort to produce solely civilian articles, such as trams, appears to have faltered in the face of difficulties in producing high-quality items at competitive prices. The diminished revenues contribute to other strains within Ukraine's aerospace industry as *Yuzhnoye* is responsible for providing its workforce and their families with basic social services. This adds an important dimension to the economic imperative for managers to find new revenue sources.

Domestic Political Support

Although it faces major economic challenges, *Yuzhnoye* benefits from strong domestic political support. Numerous high-ranking government officials have extensive work experience from the various Dnipropetrovsk enterprises or from the larger aerospace industry. In fact, Ukraine's most powerful political figure, President Kuchma, headed *Yuzhnoye* for 11 years earlier in his career. Some observers have noted that Ukraine's executive branch is dominated by a group of officials associated with Dnipropetrovsk and the country's southern industrial region.[3] But even without these personal connections, the industry enjoys substantial national backing for at least two reasons: national pride and economic necessity.

The aerospace enterprises and their past technical accomplishments are a source of national pride. Ukrainian officials are quick to note that *Yuzhnoye* and related enterprises designed and manufactured over 400 military and civilian satellites and produced several of the most advanced Soviet intercontinental ballistic missiles (ICBMS) and space boosters. Some Ukrainian officials and industry managers contend that their country's space systems incorporate designs and technologies equal or superior to those used by other space powers. The *Zenit* SLV has impressed Western aerospace experts with its highly automated launch operations and use of rocket propellants that minimise the negative impact on the environment. Such international recognition supports the strong sense of pride that many Ukrainian leaders have in their country's aerospace industry and reinforces their determination to preserve and make use of these firms and skilled workforce to help rejuvenate the Ukrainian economy.

Second, and most importantly, national leaders want to take advantage of Ukraine's strength in commercial launch capabilities and other space technologies to generate export revenues. While such financial gains have yet to occur, the high expectations of political leaders and industry managers partly account for Kiev's interest in key Ukrainian aerospace enterprises breaking into the international market.

Proliferation Risks

Irresponsible exports by these key enterprises could contribute to global proliferation in several ways. The government could decide to authorise the sale of complete systems to foreign countries even though this is prohibited by various arms-control agreements. A more likely channel for proliferation involves transferring sensitive dual-use technologies and missile-related expertise to countries seeking external assistance in manufacturing their own weapons. Such transfers could involve key subcomponents, such as guidance system mechanisms, or the specialised machinery, materials and knowledge required to produce reliable propulsion systems. Finally, there is a risk that sensitive items or missile expertise could be transferred to foreign parties through unauthorised or even inadvertent transactions.

Ukraine has made important progress in passing legislation and setting administrative regulations for governing the export activities of aerospace enterprises under the direction of the government's Expert-Technical Committee. Foreign donors, particularly the US and the UK, are providing significant technical and financial assistance to Ukraine to develop its export-control mechanisms. But the state's fledging monitoring system still concerns outside experts. Unlike Russia, Ukraine did not inherit an extensive bureaucratic apparatus for managing and scrutinising technology transfers. Even though extensive controls have been formulated by the government, these guidelines have yet to be passed into law by the Ukrainian parliament, the Rada.

Ukraine has made important progress in passing legislation

Although Ukraine's missile and space enterprises, including *Yuzhnoye*, do not appear to have blatantly flouted the MTCR restrictions in their international dealings, certain developments have raised questions about Kiev's commitment to implementing effective technology-control mechanisms. In addition, Ukraine's decision to become a formal member of the MTCR regime has been complicated by disagreements with the US over what Ukraine regards as acceptable admission requirements.

A Technology Leakage Problem?

A series of reports have suggested that Ukrainian officials have not tried hard enough to stop the leakage of missile-related technologies, expertise or even complete systems from its aerospace industry. One incident suggests that Ukraine has been helping Iraq in its efforts to resurrect a ballistic-missile capability.[4] According to a subsequent press report, US intelligence analysts believe that some Ukrainian officials have concluded an agreement to supply Libya with either SS-21 or *Scud*-B short-range ballistic missiles that Ukraine inherited from the Soviet Union.[5] Such transfers would be inconsistent with Kiev's 1994 pledge to abide by the MTCR restrictions on missile exports.[6] Selling advanced weapons to Libya would also threaten to undermine US Congressional support for technical and financial assistance to Ukraine.

Other episodes suggest that Ukraine has a mixed record on establishing effective leakage controls. One early success occurred in mid-1993 when Ukrainian officials impounded some 80 tonnes of ammonium perchlorate reportedly headed for Libya.[7] This chemical, which is useful for producing solid propellant rocket motors, was apparently produced by a Russian enterprise but was being shipped through Ukraine.

However, several subsequent incidents have raised questions about Kiev's commitment to controlling its missile technologies and expertise. In 1995, Kiev deported a group of visiting Chinese experts who were allegedly attempting to gain access to sensitive missile information during a visit to *Yuzhnoye* facilities. Although Ukraine's action indicates its desire to prevent such knowledge from falling into foreign hands, its reassurance value was largely undermined when Ukrainian security officials, who had initiated the investigation leading to the expulsion of the Chinese delegation, were subsequently relieved of their duties for reportedly embarrassing senior officials in Kiev.[8] Not long afterwards, in mid-1996, Washington undertook *démarches* to the Ukrainian and Russian governments, cautioning them about Chinese interest in acquiring advanced missile technologies associated with the large Soviet SS-18 ICBM, which is capable of delivering multiple independently targetable re-entry vehicles (MIRVs).[9] Finally, *Yuzhnoye* has allegedly permitted its missile experts to travel abroad to make their expertise available to foreign countries, without the knowledge of Ukraine's export-control officials.[10] These continuing reports raise doubts among Western non-proliferation experts about Kiev's commitment to implementing effective export controls. They also give credence to the charges that Ukraine is in danger of becoming a source of sensitive missile technologies for China and other proliferators, such as Libya.[11]

> *Ukraine is in danger of becoming a source of sensitive missile technologies*

MTCR Membership Problems

Ukraine's missile non-proliferation policies have been a major issue for countries such as the US that are seeking to control proliferation in developing countries by securing the commitment of potential technology suppliers to follow a robust MTCR regime. Although Kiev has pledged to become a formal party to the MTCR, its progress has been stalled by a serious disagreement between Kiev and Washington over the conditions for membership. If left unresolved, the continuing impasse could threaten Ukraine's progress towards its non-proliferation and commercial space objectives by reducing international backing for its activities in these inter-related areas.

Ukraine's involvement with the MTCR began in 1992 when the US began urging Kiev to adhere to the regime's guidelines on constraining exports of missiles, technologies and subcomponents that could contribute to ballistic- or cruise-missile proliferation. The two countries reached an agreement in May 1994 committing Ukraine to abide by the MTCR provisions and to implement updated export controls on missile-related technologies. (See Table 2.) This was an important step towards Ukraine becoming a formal MTCR member, which Washington had linked to US–Ukrainian co-

operation on civilian and commercial space activities. The 1994 US–
Ukraine Memorandum of Understanding (MOU) on the Transfer of
Missile Equipment and Technology pledges both countries to follow
MTCR guidelines to restrict the sale or transfer of missiles and
equipment, as well as to deny any transfer of so-called 'Category I'
items (complete missile systems, major subsystems, guidance
systems and production facilities) relevant to acquiring offensive
military missiles capable of delivering a 500kg payload over 300km.[12]
But since then, Ukraine's progress towards becoming a formal MTCR
member has been hampered by a disagreement between Washington
and Kiev over the criteria for Ukrainian membership.

The root of the US–Ukrainian impasse is a basic policy
disagreement over what Washington requires of new MTCR members.
Concerned that some countries could desire MTCR membership to
gain access to missile technologies that otherwise would be denied
them as non-members, Washington decided in 1993 to impose some
additional requirements for membership. These criteria included
being members in good standing of other non-proliferation regimes
and implementing effective export controls. But Washington also
insists that new members must forego developing or deploying their
own 'Category I' missile systems.[13] This is controversial because the
express purpose of the MTCR is to coordinate export-control efforts
rather than to impose arms-control limits on its members' missile
inventories. However, many countries, including Argentina, Brazil,
Hungary and South Africa, have accepted this precondition to gain
MTCR membership even though it involved giving up missile
programmes. Washington has made only two exceptions: one for
Russia, which became an MTCR member in 1995; and the other is
potentially for China, which remains outside the MTCR even though
it claims to adhere to an earlier set of guidelines.

Washington's position has drawn a strongly negative reac-
tion from Kiev. Ukrainian officials argue that their country is
unwilling to forego development of these types of missile systems,
which they assert could be needed to meet Ukraine's future defence
requirements.[14] Assuming that Ukraine abides by the Intermediate-
range Nuclear Forces (INF) Treaty, this means that Kiev does not
wish to foreclose the option of developing and deploying missile
systems capable of reaching 300–500km. And while claiming not to

Table 2 *Ukraine's Participation in Missile Control Accords*

International Agreements	Key Provisions and Obligations	Ukraine's Participation
Arms Reduction Treaties START 1	Limits ICBMs and SLBMs; prohibits their transfer to other countries, allows for conversion of missiles to serve as SLVs with conditions	Accepted START 1 obligations under the Lisbon Protocol and Trilateral Agreement
Missile Supplier Controls MTCR	Strong presumption against transferring complete missiles, key subsystems, production facilities, as well as guidelines for transfers of missile-related technologies and materials	Adhering to regime standards while seeking formal membership
US criteria for approving new MTCR members (23 September 1993) presidential policy	New members must renounce Category I missile programs, have effective missile export controls, and be a member in good standing of various non-proliferation agreements	Ukraine rejects restrictions on its Category I missile options

Table 2 continued

International Agreements	Key Provisions and Obligations	Ukraine's Participation
Missile Supplier Controls continued		
MOU (13 May 1994)	Ukraine pledged to abide by MTCR standards in considering any missile or space-related exports	Co-signatory
Export Controls		
Wassenaur Arrangement (12 July 1996)	New multi-national regime for transfers of conventional arms and sensitive dual-use goods and technologies	Member
Cabinet of Ministers' Decree No. 563 (27 July 1995)	Ukrainian government guidelines on the export, import or transit of missile technologies and items	National regulations but has not yet been approved by Rada

have any current plans or funds to acquire such a weapons system, they also contend that Ukraine should have the right to develop and deploy such systems as an MTCR member.

Although the particular reasons for Ukraine's adamant position on this issue is somewhat ambiguous, the result has been to halt its progress in becoming an MTCR member. Concern over its perceived international standing might play a large part in Kiev's objections to US insistence that Ukraine forego developing and deploying certain types of missile systems while not requiring Russia to accept the same. Of course, Ukrainian officials and missile designers take great pride in their country's role in producing the ICBMs and satellite systems that were integral to the former Soviet Union's military might. Their tendency to equate space power with military missiles helps to explain their insistence on having rights equal to other leading space powers, including the right under the MTCR to develop and deploy longer-range missiles. But actually acquiring such missiles is a questionable use of Ukraine's limited defence resources given that, as an MTCR member, Kiev would be prohibited from selling such missiles abroad. Furthermore, any new Ukrainian missile deployments would certainly inject more friction into its already uneasy political relationship with the Russian Federation, on which Kiev depends heavily for its energy resources.

Yuzhnoye and Ukraine's Space Programme

Kiev is actively pursuing a national space programme not only to generate much-needed hard currency, but also to gain international recognition for Ukraine as a world-class space power. As the country's largest and best-known space technology enterprise, *Yuzhnoye* is expected to play a prominent role in pursuing these twin national objectives. But given Ukraine's economic difficulties, its prospects for success will largely depend on a high degree of international cooperation.

An Ambitious Space Programme

Ukraine's space programme benefits from the active role of its political leaders in pursuing international cooperation in both the civilian and commercial space arenas. Kiev is exploring multiple avenues for expanding its role in the civilian and commercial space-launch market. The country demonstrated its growing national capability to produce, launch and operate national space systems when its *Sich-1* remote-sensing satellite was launched into orbit using a *Tsyklon* booster from Russia's Plesetsk Cosmodrome in mid-1995.

Despite the symbolic significance of *Sich-1*, Ukraine's domestic demand for satellites and slvs is minimal at best. Thus, it is actively pursuing space-cooperation agreements with a several foreign governments and is promoting joint commercial ventures between its aerospace enterprises and foreign firms. One of the most active government-to-government cooperation programmes is between Ukraine's National Space Agency and the us National Aeronautics and Space Administration (NASA). This agreement was initiated in November 1994 when Presidents Clinton and Kuchma signed a bilateral accord on outer-space cooperation, clearing the way for high-profile cooperative projects such as a joint payload experiment on a future space-shuttle mission.

Ukraine is also seeking cooperation arrangements with several other space powers. It has conducted discussions with the European Space Agency (ESA), but these have yet to yield any tangible results. Opportunities for cooperation are somewhat circumscribed by Ukraine's inability to invest financially in the proposed ventures, which is usually a requirement for participation in ESA's multinational projects. Kiev is very interested in pursuing a broad range of cooperative projects with China, including the peaceful use of space for social and economic development, and is assisting China in developing an oceanographic research satellite.[15] In some cases, President Kuchma has played a significant role in finding new partners and customers for Ukraine's space technology. He led an official delegation to Argentina, Brazil and Chile in October 1995 to establish broad economic relations, including opportunities for space cooperation. Kiev is particularly interested in Brazil as a potential user of Ukraine's *Space Clipper*, an air-borne space-launch system, as well as in exploring whether Ukraine's *Tsyklon* could make use of Brazil's *Alcantara* launch site.[16]

Yuzhnoye's Commercial Prospects

Yuzhnoye's lengthy experience of manufacturing slvs underpins Ukraine's hopes for securing a niche in the highly competitive commercial space-launch market. Since it ceased producing military missiles in 1991, *Yuzhnoye's* residual production capacity has been shifted to manufacturing and modernising the *Zenit* and *Tsyklon* SLVs. Both rockets have long histories as reliable workhorses for placing Soviet (and now Russian) military and civilian payloads into orbit.

Ukraine's orders for SLVs have traditionally come from Moscow, which has relied on the *Zenit* and *Tsyklon* to launch certain types of civilian and military satellites. But Ukraine can no longer count on receiving a significant number of orders from the Russian Federation given the steady decline in the annual number of Russian space launches, as well as Moscow's decision not to use *Zenit* to deliver its required payloads for the construction of the International Space Station.[17] Moscow's decision to cut back on Ukrainian SLVs could signal a growing effort to reduce its dependence on *Yuzhnoye* while conserving Russia's limited resources for its own cash-starved space-launch enterprises. Despite the many aerospace enterprises that Ukraine inherited, some vital elements remain outside Kiev's control. For example, many components and key subsystems, such as the rocket engines for the *Zenit* and *Tsyklon* SLVs, must be provided by Russian enterprises.[18] Because it lacks a space launch site of its own, Ukraine must rely on Russia's Plesetsk centre or the Baikonur Cosmodrome in Kazakstan. However, both Russia and Ukraine desire fully autonomous space capabilities even though their limited resources necessitate that this complex interdependency continue for the foreseeable future. The close connection between aerospace enterprises in Ukraine and the Russian Federation is an important factor in *Yuzhnoye's* opportunities for breaking into the international market.

While orders from Russia are declining, Ukraine has begun to receive major contracts for launching Western commercial payloads and has become involved in joint ventures to produce new launch systems. Its first major commercial agreement is with a multinational Western satellite consortium that has awarded *Yuzhnoye* a contract to launch 36 communication satellites into low-earth orbit in 1998 using three *Zenit-2* rockets. These satellites will constitute a large portion of the planned Globalstar communications satellite constellation.[19]

Another promising commercial effort is Ukrainian participation in joint ventures with Western aerospace firms. Rockwell International has contracted with *Yuzhnoye* to promote the *Tsyklon* rocket as a low-cost means of delivering satellites into low-earth orbits. A more substantial joint venture, known as 'Sea Launch', is a partnership with the us Boeing Space and Defense Company, Russia's *RSC Energia*, Norway's *Kvaerner* and *Yuzhnoye*. Starting in 1998, it will use a sea-based platform (a self-propelled, converted oil-drilling platform) to launch satellites into geosynchronous orbits via a modified *Zenit* rocket.[20] This multinational project has already received contracts from the Loral and Hughes Space and Communications companies of the us valued at over $500 million, and has attracted international financing.

By comparison, Ukrainian interest in using converted SS-24 or SS-18 icbms as space launchers has not attracted much international support. There seem to be several reasons why proposals for using these vehicles to place civilian or commercial payloads into orbit have not been successful. First, the us and the European Union (eu) countries have discouraged using converted icbms for civilian launches because they have a strong interest in protecting their own industries from being undercut. Second, Russian plans for using converted icbms or slvs derived from military missiles, such as the *Start*-1 rocket based on the Russian SS-25 icbm, has attracted most of the limited international support for making use of modified icbms.[21] Finally, some Ukrainian plans, such as converting the large SS-18 into an slv, require extensive Russian cooperation, which is likely to be stalled in difficult financial negotiations between the two countries.

Market Opportunities and International Competition
The difficulty of breaking into and sustaining a profitable niche in the highly competitive space-launch market will be a major test for Ukraine's government and aerospace industry. Recent projections note that planned global communication satellite networks will generate a high demand for launch services. Various studies estimate that there will be a surge in the international demand for satellite launches over the next few years as new, large communication satellite constellations are placed into earth's orbit, followed

Figure 1 *Projected Commercial Market for Satellite Launches, 1995–2010*

estimated number of satellites

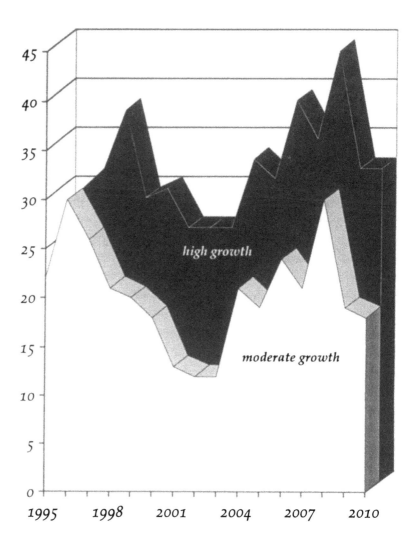

Note Launcher projections based on estimated geosynchronous transfer orbit (GTO) requirements

Source US Department of Transportation COMSTAC Report on 'Commercial Spacecraft Mission Model Update' (25 July 1996)

by a sharp decline in projected launch needs. This prospect encourages Russian and Ukrainian officials to view commercial launches as a vital source of hard currency for their struggling aerospace industries.

However, developing this niche will not be easy. For nearly a decade, most of the commercial satellite launches have been undertaken by Europe's *Arianespace* or US rockets, such as Lockheed Martin's *Atlas* and McDonnell Douglas' *Delta*. But competition in the space-launch arena is rapidly growing with entries from Brazil, China, India, Israel and Japan, as well as those from other US firms.[22]

Yuzhnoye's opportunities have been greatly bolstered by the US–Ukrainian commercial space-launch agreement that was signed in February 1996.[23] This agreement gives Ukraine some important opportunities to earn revenues as a launch provider of international satellites, which can help *Yuzhnoye* transform itself from a military missile manufacturer to an international provider of commercial space-launch services. At the same time, it strikes a balance by establishing some ground rules for Ukraine's entry into the commercial market. The agreement places quotas on the maximum number of rocket launches that Ukraine can undertake until 31 December 2001, and requires that Ukrainian space launches be offered at prices comparable to those offered by the launch firms of the market economy countries. Washington can enforce these conditions because US firms manufacture most of the world's communication satellites and supply important subcomponents to many foreign satellite manufacturers.

Refocusing the Non-Proliferation Strategy

Ukraine's aerospace industry has made substantial progress in shifting from manufacturing missiles to seeking opportunities in commercial space technologies and services. However, the transition seems to be faltering. Continuing reports of possible leakages of Ukraine's missile technologies and expertise raise questions about its willingness and capability to implement effective controls.

The international community has played a critical role in persuading Kiev to give up the nuclear weapons it inherited in favour of diplomatic acceptance, security guarantees and economic benefits. A combination of incentives and disincentives have been instrumental in encouraging Ukraine's current non-proliferation policies, but most of these external incentives and assistance programmes were originally designed to encourage its denuclearisation process or to promote the country's transition to a free market economy. The resulting patchwork of international incentives does not offer a coherent strategy for convincing managers and government officials to give high priority to missile non-proliferation, particularly while they are struggling to recapitalise the aerospace industry.

An updated non-proliferation strategy is required to promote a stronger, more demonstrable Ukrainian commitment to non-proliferation. International incentives and disincentives need to be more clearly focused on encouraging stronger controls over sensitive technologies and expertise within the aerospace industry, including *Yuzhnoye*. Concurrently, however, the non-proliferation incentive strategy must foster long-term changes in the attitudes of aerospace industry managers and government officials.

international incentives need to be more clearly focused

Both the government and industrial élite must be persuaded that their long-term interests are best served by embracing an alternate vision of Ukraine as an emerging *civilian* space power. Ukraine must show that it not only accords high priority to minimising proliferation risks in its domestic activities and international transactions, but also that it is no longer interested in deploying any type of military missile system.

Influencing Ukraine's Export Behaviour

A revised non-proliferation incentive strategy should have two short-term objectives. First, it must encourage Ukrainian industry leaders to realise that unless they pursue exports in a manner consistent with non-proliferation standards, they will not attract desirable international partners and customers. This concern with losing access to the commercial space market could be an important disincentive for them to avoid engaging in questionable export activities. Second, the international community should offer Kiev assistance to accelerate its implementation of updated controls over sensitive dual-use technologies and expertise related to manufacturing missile systems, particularly at the level of specific aerospace enterprises such as *Yuzhnoye*.

Non-proliferation Records and Commercial Opportunities

Implementing export controls at the national and enterprise levels does not come naturally for former Soviet defence industries, which are more concerned with generating exports than controlling them. But managers at *Yuzhnoye* and other aerospace enterprises must be convinced that any significant leakage of missile-related technology and expertise involves the substantial risk that they will lose foreign partners and customers. This realisation could serve as a powerful disincentive for Ukrainian enterprise managers to authorise or permit questionable transactions. Foreign governments, businesses and non-governmental organisations (NGOs) can all play an important role in convincing the managers of Ukraine's struggling aerospace industries that a good reputation for adhering to international non-proliferation norms and complying with national export controls is the best way to protect opportunities in the international space market.

Given their mutual interests as business partners in the 'Sea Launch' project, the US and Norwegian partner firms are in the best position to persuade *Yuzhnoye's* managers that a solid non-proliferation record is good for business. These foreign partners can credibly argue that reports of technology leakage or controversial exports could easily scare off foreign investors and customers. Convincing *Yuzhnoye's* managers to give non-proliferation concerns top priority would set a positive example for other Ukrainian aerospace concerns.

Export Controls and Potential

No firm evidence exists that Ukrainian aerospace enterprises, including *Yuzhnoye*, have exported sensitive missile technologies and expertise to potential proliferators. However, continuing reports of leakage suggest that serious gaps could exist or arise within Ukraine's export-control system. Some additional external assistance is probably needed to help the cash-starved aerospace enterprises move promptly to implement effective internal compliance mechanisms. If properly applied, such review procedures and in-house expertise are another important filter for alerting Ukrainian officials to the possible risks associated with outside requests for particular technology or know-how.

International assistance could play a critical role in establishing a special Ukrainian export-control centre to assist its aerospace firms in educating their managers and training their personnel on export guidelines for dual-use technologies under the MTCR and the Wassenaar Arrangement on Export Controls for Conventional Arms and Dual-Use Goods and Technologies. A good model of this type of extra-governmental organisation is the Centre on Export Controls in Moscow, which was created with official sponsorship to help Russian exporters of dual-use technologies and services adhere to the country's revised export controls.[24] International technical and financial assistance would be essential to create a similar centre in Kiev and assist with its outreach programme to help Ukrainian aerospace enterprises strengthen their internal control mechanisms.

Kiev's interest in creating such a centre could stem partly from a political desire to emulate Russia in gaining international recognition for the seriousness of its export-control efforts. However, from an economic perspective, improved controls could increase the international acceptability of the country's enterprises as potential suppliers and business partners.

Changing Ukraine's Non-Proliferation Attitudes

The existing patchwork of international incentives and assistance programmes is not rooted in a very clear concept of Ukraine's future role as a space power. An effective non-proliferation incentive strategy should seek long-term changes in the attitudes of industry élites and government officials, encouraging them to embrace an alternate vision of their country as an emerging *civilian* space power that has abandoned its military past and placed high priority on non-proliferation concerns. Two important elements in this effort concern the need to give the aerospace enterprises a growing commercial stake in establishing responsible export policies, as well as to overcome the impasse over Ukraine's admission into the MTCR. By fostering greater acceptance of non-proliferation guidelines among current government officials and enterprise managers or, alternatively, in the minds of those who succeed them, international incentives can help make Ukraine a non-proliferation exemplar.

Developing a Commercial Stake in Non-Proliferation

Washington's decision to give Ukraine access to the satellite launch market provides *Yuzhnoye* and related enterprises with a growing financial interest in avoiding activities that could undermine the opportunity to break into the international market. Encouraging the involvement of Ukrainian enterprises in joint ventures, such as the multinational 'Sea Launch' project, has the dual benefit of pairing them with Western firms that can enhance their chances for commercial success while also directly conveying the importance of abiding by non-proliferation standards in their business activities. The Western space powers should encourage the participation of *Yuzhnoye* in other space-technology ventures, including the development of a follow-on to the US Space Shuttle system and US or European plans to develop new, less costly expendable launch vehicles (ELVs). Ukraine has relevant expertise in developing SLVs, such as the *Zenit*, that feature highly automated processing and launch operations. These promise to reduce both the time and costs associated with rocket launches, and have demonstrated a high degree of reliability.[25]

the major space powers should encourage Ukrainian efforts to diversify

The major space powers should also encourage Ukrainian commercial efforts to diversify. This broader approach helps to safeguard against the possibility that Ukraine could encounter some serious setbacks in its commercial launch activities. European space enterprises could play a particularly important role in encouraging this diversification by offering joint commercial ventures and technical-assistance schemes in areas of mutual interest. These projects could draw on Ukraine's technical strengths in the space technology field, which include specialised spacecraft development, computer programming for advanced space systems and satellite sensors for remote sensing.[26]

Overcoming the MTCR Impasse

Kiev's interests are best served by showing tangible progress in the civilian and commercial space areas rather than by arguing with Washington over Ukraine's right to produce short-range missiles.

After all, any plan to deploy such missiles, which legally could be armed only with conventional warheads, would do little to enhance Ukraine's military security. Instead, it would most likely inject more friction into the already complicated relationship between Kiev and Moscow.

At the same time, Washington's insistence that Ukraine join the MTCR on the same terms as other new members who possess only limited military-missile experience and capabilities appears short-sighted at best. Although Ukraine does not fit well in the class of major space powers that possess fully autonomous capabilities for military-missile production, it resembles even less the fledgling space powers that have recently joined the MTCR.[27] Ukraine possesses missile and space-launch manufacturing facilities similar to those in the US and Russia, and it is the world's third largest producer of strategic missile systems. These considerations suggest that attempts to fit Ukraine into either category is likely to prove unsatisfactory to one party or the other. However, one possible way of overcoming this disagreement would be for Washington to support Ukraine's claim for equal standing under the MTCR to produce missiles with a range of up to 500km. This could only occur as long as Kiev understands that actually exercising this juridical right would jeopardise its prospects for international space cooperation, as well as create unnecessary complications in obtaining approval of the US licences needed to launch satellites on Ukrainian SLVs. Resolving this impasse would allow both sides to give greater attention to working together in establishing effective controls on flows of technology and expertise at both the national and aerospace enterprise levels.

Encouraging Kiev's Leadership Role

The international community has a strong non-proliferation interest in assisting Ukraine as it redefines its role as a space-technology provider. Any international incentive or disincentive offered to Kiev in this field should encourage a shift from military production to becoming a civilian space power, as well as a reliable supporter of missile non-proliferation. Ukraine could become a leader rather than a problem; it is already achieving success in the civilian and commercial areas with some assistance from the US and Europe. To the degree that it succeeds, Ukraine's experience would give a positive example to other countries, such as India, which is facing a similar problem in defining its vision as an emerging space power. It could also demonstrate the advantages that accrue to emerging technology providers adopting strong non-proliferation policies and effectively implementing them. These benefits include not only opportunities to generate foreign revenues through expanded access to the commercial space market, but also opportunities to achieve greater international standing through participation in highly visible international space cooperation ventures.

Participating in Prestigious Projects

Allowing emerging space powers like Ukraine to become involved in prestigious civilian space projects, such as the International Space Station, is one way that the global community can reward countries for forsaking military missile capabilities in favour of civilian space achievements.[28] The Space Station, currently the world's most important civilian space cooperation project, brings together Canada, ESA, Japan, the US, and, more recently, the Russian Federation. For countries like Brazil and Ukraine (and possibly India and Israel), sensitive to their international standing, developing a niche role in the Space Station project would be an important way of establishing their *bona fides* as emerging space powers and technologically advanced countries.[29] Unfortunately, while the major space powers participate in the Space Station project as partners, entailing a major financial contribution, the new space powers either have no role or are participating in lower-profile, subcontractor roles. Hence, creating some type of 'associate partner' position would offer greater opportunity to involve emerging powers in this prestigious project provided they can reliably provide some of the key skills and services.

Ukraine's role could come from its expertise in areas directly related to constructing and operating the space station, such as space welding techniques, fully automated space systems and spacecraft guidance-and-control technologies. In addition, the *Zenit* should be considered again for delivering payloads to the Space Station given Russia's difficulties, which have raised questions about whether it can fulfil its assigned role in constructing and supporting the station. Even if Ukraine's participation is only realised over a long time, developing a special connection to this prestigious programme could have a positive influence on how Ukrainian government and industry élites redefine their national identity from being a former ICBM manufacturer to a civilian space power.

With international encouragement from an effective non-proliferation incentive strategy, Ukraine could well become a leader in missile non-proliferation issues. Success in the civilian and commercial space arenas through international cooperation would set a positive example to other countries, such as India, facing a similar choice to define its long-term vision as an emerging space power. Ukraine's experience could demonstrate the advantages that accrue when emerging technology providers adopt strong non-proliferation policies. By contrast, deciding to retain or pursue military missile capabilities should be perceived as reducing opportunities for access to civilian space cooperation and commercial market access.

Giving up Military Missiles

One price Ukraine has paid in choosing to define its future as a civilian space power is to abandon current interests in military missile systems. Any effort to develop new systems would be inconsistent with this revised national commitment. In addition, the Ukrainian government should consider giving up its interest in using converted ICBMS as commercial SLVs. *Yuzhnoye's* various proposals have not attracted strong foreign interest; however, its continuing effort to use these military missiles will only cloud the international perception of it as an emerging civilian space power and distract it from succeeding as a world-class manufacturer of modern SLVs.

Even though Ukraine's aerospace industry has already shifted its priorities to emphasise civilian space technologies over manufacturing military missiles, the conversion to being a purely civilian space power would still require a major change in the attitudes of many government officials and aerospace industry élites. In addition to demonstrating its ability to implement effective controls over sensitive technologies and missile expertise, Ukraine would have to give up any remaining interests in producing military missiles or converting excess ICBMs to civilian SLVs to convince its potential international supporters of its serious commitment to responsible non-proliferation policies. International incentives, along with certain disincentives or the threat of lost incentives, can play an important role in convincing Ukrainian government officials and managers at *Yuzhnoye* and other space-technology enterprises that their country has substantial interests at stake in giving non-proliferation concerns a high priority.

chapter 3

Improving Minatom's Export Policies

Russia's Ministry of Atomic Energy (Minatom) poses a particular challenge to international efforts aimed at influencing its nuclear export activities. Minatom's interest in expanding its niche in the civilian nuclear market-place has been galvanised by severe cutbacks in government funding for producing nuclear weapons and power reactors. Its aggressive export activities, including controversial nuclear deals with China, India and Iran, threaten to exacerbate the global spread of nuclear-weapon technologies and expertise. The international community has a clear security interest in convincing Minatom's managers and the country's political leaders that decisions on nuclear exports should be based on a strong non-proliferation commitment. But any external effort faces several obstacles, such as Minatom's competing organisational priorities, and the international community's diverse and sometimes conflicting interests in assisting Russia with its nuclear problems. Nonetheless, international incentives and disincentives can play an important role in changing Russian nuclear-export behaviour in the short term, as well as in encouraging changes in the attitudes of Minatom's managers regarding the importance of non-proliferation concerns in export decisions.

Minatom as an Emerging Technology Provider

For Minatom, the days of enjoying top priority for national resources to manufacture nuclear weapons and power reactors are past. Given the Russian Federation's continuing economic difficulties, Minatom is seeking to generate much-needed hard currency by dramatically increasing its sales of nuclear-related technologies, fissile materials and fuel services to the international nuclear market.

A Mixed Soviet Legacy

Minatom inherited a mixed legacy from the Soviet nuclear industry. In its previous incarnation, the Ministry was the primary organisation for developing, producing and testing nuclear weapons.[1] It managed a wide range of design laboratories, production facilities and even nuclear testing sites that supported its nuclear-weapon responsibilities. But the end of the Cold War, which created opportunities for reducing the US and Soviet nuclear arsenals, largely obviated Minatom's previously vital military mission of manufacturing nuclear weapons. Its military activities have largely shifted from manufacturing and testing nuclear weapons to dismantling them. According to Russian officials, the Ministry of Defence is retiring nuclear weapons at a rate of about 2,000–3,000 a year.[2] Minatom dismantles the weapons and stores the fissile material products, mainly weapons-grade plutonium and HEU.

The Ministry has also been in charge of developing and constructing Russia's nuclear-power programme both at home and abroad. This mission involves broad responsibilities for managing the country's nuclear-fuel cycle: producing nuclear fuel; constructing reactors; and providing important fuel services, including uranium enrichment, reprocessing and spent-fuel storage. Although nuclear power accounts for only about 12% of Russia's overall electricity production, nuclear power stations are often an important energy source for certain regions and the primary source for some remote population centres.[3] Minatom's ambitious plans to construct additional power stations have largely stalled because of government funding shortages and the legacy of public concerns resulting from the 1986 Chernobyl reactor accident.[4] Most of Russia's efforts are now confined to upgrading the safety of earlier-generation Soviet-designed nuclear reactors and completing construction of several nuclear power stations halted in the aftermath of the Chernobyl incident. Russia's nuclear reactor programme is also experiencing major operating difficulties because of severe shortages in operating funds. This financial shortfall, greatly exacerbated by customers not paying for electricity consumption, has a deleterious effect on plant safety, morale and efficiency.[5] In addition, inadequate funding has compelled Minatom's managers to allocate their limited resources in a piecemeal fashion to cover the minimal requirements of current military and civilian operations, its workforce and facilities and work on new projects.[6]

Minatom is a highly centralised organisation with substantial human and capital resources. The core of its nuclear research and production capabilities are located in the ten closed cities that still comprise the backbone of Russia's nuclear 'archipelago'. These cities are home to the country's scientific and engineering élite who were involved in nuclear-weapon design and production or who supported various nuclear-power activities. Located in relatively isolated areas, the so-called 'secret cities', with an estimated population of nearly 700,000 workers plus their dependants, existed to support the Soviet Union's nuclear research institutes, weapons laboratories and other facilities associated with the nuclear-fuel cycle.[7] But with the steady decline of Moscow's budget allocations over the past decade, these centres have not only lost their earlier privileged position but have also fallen on desperate times.[8] Their plight only reinforces the pressure on Minatom's managers to find new sources of revenue.

Minatom's Strong Domestic Political Position

Minatom enjoys a strong domestic position in the Russian policy-making process, thus making it difficult for other executive or parliamentary actors to question the non-proliferation implications of Minatom's export decisions. This situation makes it hard to seek changes in Russian nuclear-export policies through an understanding between political leaders, the route the us and other non-proliferation supporters have often taken in the past.

Minatom is the only defence-industry ministry to survive the Soviet Union's dissolution almost wholly intact. It draws bureaucratic strength from its highly centralised and self-sufficient structure. Its critics characterise it as a 'state within a state' because of its bureaucratic autonomy and continuing control over diverse resources, such as agriculture enterprises, that fall outside its nuclear- energy missions.[9] Furthermore, since early 1992, Minatom has been headed by Minister Viktor Mikhailov, a highly experienced official who began his career in the Soviet nuclear-weapons complex nearly four decades ago. The importance of Mikhailov's political standing within the Yeltsin government was confirmed in July 1995 when he was promoted to the Security Council.[10]

Disparate Perspectives on Nuclear Power

Despite the Chernobyl disaster and the Soviet Union's dissolution, Minatom remains a powerful government advocate of expanding Russia's domestic nuclear power capabilities and enlarging its portion of the international nuclear market. Minatom officials do not share the negative view of fissile material held by many US officials and experts. From their perspective, plutonium is a valuable commodity that can provide profitable opportunities for fuel services and serve as an important long-term energy resource in the form of fuel for breeder reactors and reactors configured to burn plutonium–uranium mixed-oxide (MOX) fuel.[11]

The disparity in basic views on nuclear materials and the future importance of nuclear power has been reflected in the delays and difficulties that have plagued efforts by US and Russian nuclear officials to find cooperative solutions to various Russian nuclear issues. A difference in perspective about nuclear power has complicated efforts to devise a joint programme for disposing of large Russian stockpiles of excess weapons plutonium. After much study and debate, US and Russian officials agreed in late 1996 to consider a 'dual track' approach to dispose of this excess. They decided to pursue both the immobilisation option favoured by the US and Minatom's preferred option of converting the excess plutonium into a MOX fuel that can be burned in reactors to generate electricity.[12] Although US officials and experts have been sceptical about the MOX fuel approach, they are willing to explore it in case of problems with the immobilisation process and, equally importantly, to encourage Russia to eliminate its plutonium stockpile. Compared with US reticence, several other nuclear-power states, including Canada, France, Germany and Japan, share

Minatom remains a powerful government advocate of expanding Russia's domestic nuclear-power capabilities

Russia's enthusiasm for recycling their accumulating plutonium as a power- reactor fuel. For example, Minatom has been collaborating with Germany's Siemens and France's Cogema on designing and constructing a MOX fabrication plant in Russia that could supply the resulting fuel to specially configured power reactors.[13]

Thus, Washington and Moscow have compromised on solutions that narrow the gap in their policy preferences regarding the problems of replacing Russia's plutonium-producing reactors and disposing of its excess weapons-grade plutonium. However, the basic differences in US and Russian nuclear-energy perspectives still exist and complicate any effort to devise a coherent international strategy for influencing Minatom's nuclear-export policies.

Minatom's Drive for Nuclear Exports

Minatom appears to have adopted what might be called an 'ideology of export' in zealously seeking to generate hard currency from its nuclear exports. This new interest in exporting nuclear technologies and fuel services comes largely from its urgent need for hard currency to sustain and modernise the organisation. Despite the tarnished reputation of Soviet-designed nuclear reactors following the Chernobyl accident, Minatom still has much to offer, particularly to countries with fledging nuclear programmes. It has technical expertise and operating experience with nuclear-power reactors, as well as relatively sophisticated dual-use technologies for uranium enrichment and plutonium processing.

Moscow has been a major exporter of nuclear technologies and fuel services for several decades. During the Cold War, most of its international transactions had strong political elements and focused on Soviet allies and client states. Although the Russian nuclear industry enjoys new commercial opportunities in the Cold War's aftermath, it also faces substantial competition from established Western and emerging Asian nuclear exporters. Under these conditions, there is a significant risk that Minatom will seek a market niche by offering nuclear and dual-use technologies to countries and organisations with questionable non-proliferation records.

Minatom's export activities are diverse, including sales of raw materials, providing fuel services, reactor construction and trans-

Table 3 *Russian Nuclear Exports and Nuclear Activities*

Type of nuclear exports or cooperation activities	International customers or partners	Current status
Reactor construction and operations training	Cuba	Lack of funding to proceed
	China	1 reactor under contract
	India	Plans for 2 reactors
	Iran	Initial stages of completing unfinished, older reactor
	Slovakia	Member of multinational team to complete 2 reactors
	Ukraine	Discussions on reactor construction
Dual-use technology sales	China	Initial stages of uranium enrichment plant completed
Sale of uranium ore concentrate	world market	Russia is a top world supplier of "yellow cake" for nuclear fuel
LEU sales	Bulgaria, Finland, Hungary, Ukraine etc	Continuing supplier of reactor fuel elements

Table 3 *continued*

Type of nuclear exports or cooperation activities	International customers or partners	Current status
HEU sales	United States	Russian HEU converted to power reactor fuel for US
	Europe	Discussions about supplying HEU for research reactors
Major nuclear research and development projects	France and Germany	Mixed oxide (MOX) Production plant design, and Nuclear reactor safety systems
	Iran, China and India	Thermonuclear research Reactor development
	United States	Plutonium reactor core conversion project and plutonium disposition research

Note   Minatom relies on several special purpose organisations to perform its international trade activities. These include *Tekhsnabexport* (exports of nuclear fuel services) and *Atomenergoexport* and *Zarubezhatomenergostroi* (exports of nuclear power plant equipment and construction services).

ferring nuclear technologies and experience. (See Table 3.) Nuclear-fuel services account for about two-thirds of Minatom's foreign revenues.[14] Russian press reports credit Minatom with bringing in some $1.65bn in 1995 from its international transactions. Senior officials expect sales of nuclear-fuel services and construction of power reactor stations to increase to $2bn by 1998, with about $500m annually from constructing of nuclear-power plants in other countries.[15] Russia is also responsible for about 25% of the world's uranium production and is a major producer and exporter of uranium ore concentrate.[16]

Constructing Russian nuclear reactors in other countries is the type of export that attracts the greatest international attention. Along with attempts to secure a role in building nuclear-power stations in Central Europe, such as helping to complete Slovakia's Soviet-designed reactors at Mochovic, Minatom officials are pursuing what they see as new commercial opportunities in the international market, particularly in Asia. But efforts to expand Russia's niche have not been an unequivocal success despite some notable deals. Minatom has negotiated agreements with China, Cuba, India and Iran to construct or complete nuclear power reactors and provide various training and fuel services.[17] Russia is also constructing a uranium enrichment facility in China. However, more advanced nuclear powers, such as Japan and South Korea, are less interested in receiving Russian technology and services than in developing their own indigenous nuclear capabilities and eventually becoming exporters themselves. Russia has also been unable to secure a significant role in the Korean Peninsula Energy Development Organisation (KEDO), the multi-national project to supply North Korea with two new light water reactors (LWRs) in exchange for Pyongyang's commitment to halt operations in nuclear facilities suspected of supporting a nuclear-weapons programme.

Minatom appears to have an 'ideology of export'

Thus, Minatom's almost desperate efforts to become an international technology provider raise significant non-proliferation concerns. Some experts fear that this economic pressure will cause Minatom's managers, and even Russia's political leaders, to discount the risks of exporting sensitive dual-use technologies and expertise to foreign customers with questionable reputations rather than lose lucrative opportunities to secure contracts and earn hard currency.

Proliferation Risks

Minatom has major national responsibilities for seeing that Russian fissile material, nuclear-related technologies and weapon expertise do not exacerbate the weapon-proliferation problem either through internal leakage or through questionable export activities. While the international community has focused its efforts on assisting the Russian Federation with security measures that address the 'loose nukes' problem, much less consensus exists on Minatom's questionable exports and the role that foreign countries should play in encouraging more responsible export policies.

Risks of Nuclear Leakage

Non-proliferation experts are particularly concerned with the disposition of weapons-grade fissile material, namely plutonium and HEU, considered the most important component for a nuclear-weapon capability. The Soviet Union's rapid political and economic collapse increased international perceptions of the 'loose nukes' problem. The unprecedented flow of nuclear weapons and fissile materials, which has resulted from the ongoing process of dismantling substantial numbers of former strategic and tactical nuclear weapons in Russia and other former Soviet states, increases the chances for leakage. The need to provide storage and adequate security for the fissile materials resulting from the dismantlement of up to 3,000 nuclear weapons each year appears to have outstripped Minatom's available resources.[18]

Uncertainty over the adequacy of nuclear security arrangements at Minatom facilities and nuclear research institutes has generated international concern about the risk of smuggling at these facilities, including unauthorised diversion or theft with insider assistance. Many experts have noted that Minatom lacks the strong security culture of its Western counterparts. The earlier Soviet approach mostly focused on securing facilities against external threats instead of providing adequate physical protection within nuclear sites and introducing material-accounting systems to detect insider theft.[19] While the security of nuclear weapons under the supervision of the Russian Ministry of Defence is considered relatively high, continuing smuggling incidents involving nuclear material, including some small amounts of weapons-grade material, have highlighted Minatom's shortfalls in instituting effective protection and material accounting measures.

The depth of international concern over Russia's internal controls is reflected in the various cooperative programmes that have been initiated to help improve its nuclear-material protection and safety practices. In April 1996 in Moscow, the Group of Seven (G-7) industrialised nations plus the Russian Federation agreed to a multi-faceted programme involving rigorous national measures to protect and account for fissile material. The summit declaration called for increased international cooperation to combat illicit trafficking in these materials. This cooperation is to include greater inter-governmental coordination and information exchanges about significant cases of nuclear smuggling.[20]

plans to build reactors or to sell sensitive nuclear technologies to China, India and Iran are worrisome

Risks from Irresponsible Nuclear Exports

Russia's political leaders are unlikely to approve any Minatom plan for nuclear exports that is clearly inconsistent with the Russian Federation's obligations under the NPT or various export-control agreements, such as the NSG. However, nuclear-export questions often fall between the letter of formal obligations and the spirit of these non-proliferation agreements. International supporters of a robust non-proliferation regime contend that responsible countries must exhibit a certain degree of self-restraint. This often means avoiding transferring sensitive dual-use technologies and expertise to countries with questionable non-proliferation reputations, even if such actions are not legally prohibited. Hence, irresponsible technology transfers could contribute to the weapons-proliferation problem in several ways.

First, the recipient country might import foreign nuclear technologies and expertise ostensibly to support its civilian nuclear programme while directly or indirectly exploiting these imports to bolster progress on a covert weapons programme. In this situation, civilian nuclear activities essentially serve as a façade to reduce international concern that an illegal programme exists. Prior to the 1991 Gulf War, Iraq followed a dual-track approach, pursuing a nuclear- weapons capability under the cover of a civilian nuclear programme.[21]

Second, the proliferation risk could be increased if legal nuclear transfers allow a recipient to acquire illegal technologies or know-how. Particularly in cases where the technology provider has a pressing need for hard currency, there could be lucrative opportunities for transferring sensitive technologies and expertise. There is also always the possibility that illegal transactions could result from the unauthorised actions of low-level personnel on both sides who are in frequent contact. However, a more serious possibility involves sensitive transfers that occur with the tacit approval of enterprise managers whose personal or organisational interests lead them to overlook, or even encourage, these questionable activities. Illegal or highly questionable transfers might even be seen as necessary 'sweeteners' for finalising a major deal.

Third, the recipient of such transfers could exacerbate the proliferation problem by passing on nuclear technology, material or expertise to other proliferators. In effect, this 'two-step' process would increase the likelihood that sensitive technologies, such as those associated with uranium enrichment or plutonium proces-sing, could be obtained by problem countries with few alternative sources for acquiring nuclear-related items.

Finally, a nuclear-supplier country could undercut inter-national efforts to persuade certain countries to become NPT members and accept the associated obligations. This is particularly relevant where a supplier is willing to provide technology or expertise to non-NPT members, such as India and Pakistan, which refuse to accept full-scale safeguards on their entire nuclear infrastructures.

Questionable Minatom Nuclear Exports

From a non-proliferation perspective, Minatom's plans to build reactors or to sell sensitive nuclear technologies to Iran, China and India are probably the most worrisome cases. In one way or another, these countries have exhibited questionable commitments to non-proliferation. In addition, uncertainty exists over the Russian government's commitment and capability to control sensitive dual-use nuclear-technology exports.

The Russia–Iran Nuclear Deal

Russia's agreement to support Iran's fledgling nuclear programme has provoked great international concern and debate. In 1995 Minatom signed an $800m contract with the Atomic Energy Organisation of Iran (AEOI) to complete an unfinished nuclear reactor at Bushehr. Minatom also agreed to train Iranian specialists and to provide the necessary nuclear-fuel services. Subsequent discussions have focused on the possibility that Russia might build additional power reactors in Iran. The Russia–Iran nuclear deal has become a continuing point of disagreement between Washington and Moscow. US officials have repeatedly urged Yeltsin and Prime Minister Viktor Chernomyrdin to cancel these agreements with Iran.[22] Moscow has categorically rejected Washington's argument, arguing that:

- Iran is a signatory to the NPT;
- it has agreed to full-scale IAEA nuclear safeguards;
- Iran has successfully passed several IAEA inspections to date;
- Russia has agreed to reprocess the spent fuel that these reactors will produce; and
- the reactor that Russia has sold to Iran is basically the same type as the LWR that Washington supports for sale to North Korea.[23]

But US officials and experts are not convinced by such arguments; they suspect that Tehran intends to exploit its public nuclear programme to conceal and support a covert effort to acquire nuclear weapons.[24]

Observers have also been worried by reports that Minatom officials were willing to sell gas centrifuge enrichment technology to Iran. Although this dual-use equipment can be used to enrich reactor fuel, it is also closely linked to producing the HEU needed for nuclear weapons. Reports that Minatom officials offered this sensitive technology to Iran without apprising other Russian government agencies, including the Ministry of Foreign Affairs, of their plans are particularly disturbing. In response to US protests,

Yeltsin pledged in May 1995 at the US–Russian summit in Moscow to eliminate enrichment technologies from Russia's nuclear deal with Iran.[25] Nonetheless, this incident is viewed by some Western experts as emblematic of Minatom's willingness to export sensitive technologies and the reluctance of Russian political leaders to impose strict controls on exports that promise to bring in substantial foreign revenues.

Nuclear-Reactor Sales to India

Minatom's negotiations with India to construct nuclear reactors also raise questions about Russia's non-proliferation commitment.[26] Moscow seeks approval from the other members of the NSG by claiming the right to proceed with this project because it originated prior to Moscow's NSG membership. But many countries want to deny exports to threshold nuclear-weapon countries, such as India, as a way of pressuring them into renouncing their weapon programmes and joining the non-proliferation regime. From this perspective, Russian willingness to supply nuclear technologies and services to India threatens to undermine this international policy by encouraging New Delhi to remain outside the non-proliferation regime.

Building a Uranium Enrichment Plant in China

Minatom has agreed to sell gas centrifuge technology for enriching uranium to China, which the Ministry views as a potentially important market for its nuclear technologies and services.[27] Given China's questionable reputation in this area, sensitive uranium enrichment technologies could find its way into the hands of proliferation problem countries, such as Iran or Pakistan, through a two-step process. Although Russian officials claim to have placed certain limits on the technology and expertise associated with the project, China's industries have historically exhibited great skill in reverse-engineering foreign technical designs. Chinese enterprises could exploit Russian technologies to manufacture their own gas centrifuges for both domestic use and foreign sales.

Questionable Controls Over Sensitive Technologies

Russia has a well-developed set of national export controls at least on paper; substantial progress has been made in generating related presidential decrees and passing national legislation.[28] However, a continuing weakness involves controlling the flow of sensitive technologies and information among the former Soviet republics. This creates opportunities for leakage via inter-republic sales that eventually make their way to foreign customers.

There are also indications that some Russian entrepreneurs are actively seeking to sell sensitive nuclear technologies without considering their potential implications for weapons proliferation. Advertisements which have appeared in a Moscow daily newspaper to sell extractors and centrifuges are believed to reflect the lack of a strong nuclear safeguard culture among newly privatised Russian technology enterprises eager to generate revenues.[29]

Existing Programmes and Incentives

The Russian Federation receives a significant amount of assistance from foreign donors for key military and civilian nuclear problem areas. Only a few of the many international programmes designed to help Moscow are directly related to encouraging more responsible export policies. The other cooperative programmes focus mainly on improving safety and security, as well as eliminating excess nuclear forces. Although they usually take the form of direct financial and technical assistance, such programmes also offer implicit incentives for Moscow to cooperate in these areas of international concern.

Promoting Responsible Exports

The most effective international programmes designed to encourage Russia to be a responsible exporter focus on strengthening its nuclear export controls. In addition, a us–Russian commercial nuclear trade agreement signed in 1994, known as the HEU deal, provides a potentially important means for Minatom to generate foreign revenues through fissile-material exports that are compatible with a robust non-proliferation posture.

The us, the UK and others are providing technical assistance to the Russian Federation to improve its customs enforcement mechanisms so that its exports meet various non-proliferation guidelines, including those formulated by the NSG and the Zangger Committee.[30] These governments and various NGOs have also supported the Centre for Export Controls in Moscow, a quasi-governmental organisation that seeks to strengthen the awareness and compliance of Russia's dual-use technology enterprises, particularly those in the private sector, with the full range of Russia's export obligations.

The HEU deal gives Minatom a potentially profitable contract to supply the US with reactor fuel produced by blending down HEU from dismantled Soviet nuclear weapons. Under this contract, Minatom could earn up to $12bn over the next two decades by converting 500m tonnes of HEU material into more than 15,000m tonnes of low-enriched uranium (LEU) fuel for use in US power reactors.[31] Recent contract modifications have removed some impediments in the original US–Russian arrangement that created substantial uncertainty about the price and quantity of nuclear shipments Minatom could expect from the United States Enrichment Corporation (USEC), a government-owned corporation in the process of being privatised.[32] The agreement is also being modified to allow Russia to receive advance payments from USEC for future deliveries of nuclear fuel.

Other Assistance Programmes

A large portion of the international nuclear-related assistance in the Russian Federation helps eliminate excess nuclear forces and protects and secures the large amounts of fissile material being generated by this elimination and other military-related sources. US assistance is provided through the CTR programme set up to help dismantle, securely transport and safely destroy nuclear weapons and their associated strategic delivery systems. Funding and equipment transfers supporting these cooperative activities come largely from the US and, to a lesser degree, from other nuclear-weapons countries, such as the UK.

The US has also taken the lead in helping Minatom upgrade security arrangements for Russia's weapons-usable nuclear materials in programmes aimed at enhancing the protection, control and accounting (MPC&A) of weapons-grade fissile material at Russian research institutes and other facilities involved in producing nuclear weapons.[33] The US Department of Energy's government-to-government programme to improve nuclear protection and security at key Minatom facilities has made slow progress because of Russian suspicions about US motives in seeking access to sensitive nuclear facilities.[34] In comparison, its lab-to-lab programme has achieved much greater success, using an approach that features joint projects teaming scientists at US and Russian weapons laboratories to develop MPC&A enhancements for specific Russian facilities. This 'bottom up' approach offers much greater flexibility for both sides to overcome bureaucratic obstacles by devising expedient solutions to the MPC&A needs at a specific facility.[35]

Another potentially important nuclear cooperative programme focuses on international efforts to improve the uncertain safety of the 58 Soviet-designed civilian power reactors located in the former Soviet republics and Central Europe.[36] Although the US provides much of the assistance for dismantling nuclear weapons and securing fissile material, support for dealing with reactor safety and waste handling involves a much broader range of international participation, including from Japan and European states. The Europeans perceive a more direct stake in these situations on their borders and have more experience and technical assistance to offer on civil nuclear problems. As well as numerous bilateral activities, a multinational programme for funding safety improvements at reactors and staff training is being administered by the European Bank for Reconstruction and Development (EBRD).[37] Nonetheless, little progress has been made in improving safety practices and shutting down questionable reactors; Russia and other former Soviet republics are reluctant to give up these energy-producing power reactors in favour of expensive replacement projects, unless extensive foreign funding is forthcoming.

The Russian Federation is receiving technical and financial assistance from the international community to help with a broad range of military and civilian nuclear activities. Unfortunately, however, these programmes are more a patchwork than a coherent strategy for encouraging Moscow to pursue responsible nuclear-export policies.

Influencing Minatom's Export Behaviour

The international community must re-orient its approach if it wants Moscow to adopt a stronger non-proliferation policy in its nuclear exports. Incentives can play an important part in an updated strategy by presenting Minatom's managers with clearer advantages and disincentives that highlight the significant political and economic costs of making questionable nuclear exports. Any revised strategy should seek to improve Minatom's export behaviour in the near term while aiming to change the attitudes of its managers in the long run to give greater priority to non-proliferation concerns. Influencing Minatom's export behaviour will require linking Russia's economic opportunities in the international nuclear market to certain obligations, such as implementing rigorous nuclear technology-export controls, and foregoing the foreign sale of uranium-enrichment and plutonium- processing technologies. A combination of incentives and disincentives directly relevant to Minatom's high-priority projects are essential to convince its managers of the commercial and technological returns that come from exercising greater self-restraint.

Greater Self-Restraint in Nuclear Exports

Moscow can strengthen its non-proliferation approach by controlling exports, particularly those involving the numerous enterprises that design and manufacture sensitive dual-use technologies. Minatom should be held responsible for helping national authorities monitor dual-use technology exports made by newly privatised enterprises that have, or once had, access to sensitive technologies and expertise for manufacturing nuclear weapons or weapons-grade fissile material.

Similarly, international incentives and disincentives should be used to discourage Minatom from selling uranium-enrichment and plutonium-processing technologies on the international market. Minatom should demonstrate that unauthorised leakage is occurring neither at its institutes and manufacturing plants nor through privatised firms that are – or once were – connected to it. It should be encouraged to adopt a policy that emphasises providing nuclear-fuel services rather than sensitive technology sales to foreign customers. Even older- generation technologies, such as the early gas centrifuges, could be useful to proliferators seeking to produce weapons-grade fissile material. A Russian policy decision to refrain from transferring sensitive technology to any foreign customers, including enterprises in other former Soviet republics, would greatly diminish the risk that recipient countries, such as China, could acquire such technology and later sell derivative models to countries with questionable non-proliferation reputations, such as Pakistan and Iran.

Encouraging changes in Minatom's export behaviour requires measures specifically targeted at those managers expanding the firm's niche in the nuclear market. In terms of incentives, Minatom must be convinced that responsible export behaviour will improve its chances of receiving foreign cooperation on development projects of great interest to its directors, such as a MOX-fuel production facility. In terms of disincentives, managers must also be convinced that failing to give non-proliferation concerns a high priority when making export decisions could damage their prospects for obtaining hard currency through the US–Russian HEU deal.

MOX-Fuel Production

The US and Russian agreement to pursue a 'dual-track approach' to dispose of excess weapons-grade plutonium also gives the enterprise a greater organisational stake in exhibiting responsible nuclear-export behaviour. To succeed in a timely manner, the multinational project will require extensive scientific studies and substantial funding for the various facilities needed to convert the plutonium 'pits' into an oxide form and to produce the MOX assemblies.[38] But France, Germany, the US and other possible foreign supporters of a major programme to expand Minatom's infrastructure for producing MOX fuel should agree to make their continuing financial and technical assistance conditional on an unambiguous Russian commitment to responsible nuclear export policies.

Without this international cooperation and financial support, Minatom's plans are unlikely to be realised. Thus, foreign supporters should link their participation in this or any other programme to its behaviour as an emerging technology provider. A clear message must be conveyed to Minatom's directors that only a responsible nuclear exporter can expect to receive funding from financial institutions such as the EBRD.

Follow-on HEU Contracts

Another way to encourage responsible nuclear-export policies by the Russian Federation is through agreements that allows Minatom to generate significant foreign revenues from countries with good non-proliferation reputations. By far the most important of these agreements is the 1993 HEU agreement calling for Russia to provide the US with nuclear-power reactor fuel blended down from HEU taken from former Soviet nuclear weapons.[39] This agreement, with its substantial $12bn return, could be presented as an alternative to Minatom's pursuit of questionable nuclear exports, such as the $800m nuclear reactor deal for Iran.

Although the original HEU deal contained provisions that devalued its advantage for Minatom, subsequent modifications have bolstered its potential to influence the Ministry's executives in terms of providing a reliable and substantial source of hard currency. If the terms of the US–Russian agreement had been completely set for the next two decades, then this arrangement could probably not exert much influence over Minatom's export decisions. However, the present contract only sets the terms for Russian nuclear-fuel deliveries to the US for five of the agreement's anticipated 20-year duration. The US government is likely to play an important role in formulating any subsequent agreement between Minatom and the USEC, as well as resolving specific financial questions that arise during implementation.

The need to renew the HEU contract gives Minatom's managers an important disincentive for allowing sensitive Russian nuclear technologies and expertise to be obtained by countries with questionable non-proliferation commitments. By making these transactions, Minatom risks political 'complications' arising when the nuclear-fuel contract with the USEC is reviewed, or the US Congress imposing conditions that preclude renewing the contract as long as Minatom is a party to controversial exports.

Changing Minatom's Attitudes

As well as influencing Minatom's export behaviour in the short term, a major reason for including incentives in a revised international strategy would be to encourage a long-term change in the attitudes of Minatom's managers and key subgroups towards non-proliferation concerns when making export decisions. Using economic and technical incentives, these groups could be given a greater stake in responsible non-proliferation behaviour, particularly in terms of exercising self-restraint in Russia's nuclear-export activities.

This revised strategy would be designed to convince Minatom's directors that responsible export decisions are good business. Various initiatives could be integral to this strategy. But these opportunities should be made conditional on Minatom's willingness to forego questionable nuclear-export projects. Such conditions would require Moscow to curtail its controversial nuclear dealings with Iran and to abandon any plans to build nuclear reactors for New Delhi unless that country makes a commitment to the NPT.

Curtailing Questionable Projects

Regardless of the merits of each argument, the Iranian nuclear debate could become a political time bomb, threatening a showdown in US–Russian relations. This issue could acquire growing US domestic political saliency as Russia progresses on its 55-month schedule to complete the Bushehr nuclear reactor. Similarly, Minatom's agreement to build new reactors is also likely to raise concerns about the wisdom of assisting an organisation that seems to pursue unrestrained nuclear- export policies. Thus, linking Minatom's controversial export policies and international assistance could undermine the US domestic political base for funding work aimed at improving Russian nuclear security and safety.

Given Iran's economic difficulties and internal political turmoil, it is questionable whether the Bushehr project will ever be completed. Using Russian technology to finish a power station that was originally based on a very different German reactor design is a dubious proposition at best. This project is almost impossible to complete as long as Bonn prohibits *Kraftwerk Union* (KWU), the German nuclear- contracting firm, from releasing the original construction data, despite Iran's threats to bring legal action against the various German enterprises originally involved in the project.[40]

Minatom's interest in proceeding with this complex project is likely to diminish rapidly if Iran begins cutting off funding because of intractable technical problems. However, even if the plant is never completed, Minatom enterprises and their Iranian counterpart organisations could devise other joint projects to permit the sale of Russian nuclear technologies, materials and expertise.[41] The international community should be prepared to offer Minatom's managers and Russian political leaders a better alternative and new opportunities to become involved in joint and multinational ventures with other nuclear suppliers, provided Moscow is willing to forego these other transactions. To help reassure the international community that Minatom is not transferring sensitive technologies and nuclear know-how, Moscow should abandon major nuclear projects, such as constructing nuclear reactors in Iran and adopt transparency measures that will permit outside experts to assess more accurately the extent of the firm's official contacts.

Joint Ventures

One incentive to help change the attitudes of Russian nuclear officials over the long run is joint ventures between Minatom and foreign firms in both the commercial nuclear market, which can generate work and revenues for the Russian nuclear industry, and in developing new power reactors, which is essential for sustaining its scientific and technical talent. Although Minatom's managers perceive substantial commercial opportunities to secure contracts to build new power reactors, particularly among the East Asian countries, Russian reactors have limited appeal to those who can afford to go elsewhere. The experience in the aerospace area suggests that joint ventures are an effective means for bringing former Soviet defence enterprises into the market economy rapidly while conveying the good business sense of a responsible export record.[42]

In an effort to overcome its negative reputation created by the Chernobyl incident, Minatom has entered into joint ventures with German and French nuclear enterprises to provide improved instrumentation and safety systems for Russian nuclear reactors. For example, the Ministry is involved in a consortium of foreign enterprises including *Franatome* and Siemens to complete Slovakia's nuclear-power station at Mochovic.[43] If this joint project produces a relatively safe and reliable power station, it could set an encouraging precedent regarding the mutual benefits of commercial joint ventures.

These ventures should be encouraged to enhance the safety and performance of any new Russian nuclear-power reactors. For Minatom to obtain foreign revenues by constructing safe and efficient nuclear-power stations abroad is preferable to less safe reactors being built by other Russian enterprises while Minatom offers more sensitive nuclear technologies, such as modern uranium enrichment, to potential proliferators. At the same time, foreign firms are likely to benefit from having Minatom as a partner when they seek contracts to complete or modernise nuclear-power stations in Russia and Central Europe, given that the original reactors were designed mainly by Minatom's research institutes and built by its construction force.[44]

The US–Russian lab-to-lab programme for upgrading nuclear security at Russian facilities is an important model for under-standing how the attitudes of Minatom officials and scientists at specific enterprises can change through cooperative ventures. Encouraging joint ventures between Minatom and foreign enterprises with proven non-proliferation records could also strengthen the advocacy role of important Minatom subgroups trying to avoid irresponsible nuclear export policies. Mid-level officials involved in these joint ventures might also broadly accept non-proliferation as an organisational priority within the firm through their dealings with colleagues and as they advance to positions of greater responsibility.

Encouraging Russian Involvement in KEDO

Assuming that Moscow eventually drops its controversial plans to build nuclear reactors for Iran and India, or if these complicated deals simply fall through, the international community should encourage the Russian Federation to become much more involved in KEDO. This organisation was created by Japan, South Korea and the US to implement the October 1994 Agreed Framework, which calls for constructing two LWRs in North Korea in exchange for Pyongyang eliminating nuclear facilities and spent fuel that is suspected of supporting its nuclear weapons acquisitions effort.[45]

Minatom should provide fuel services for KEDO

KEDO's membership is steadily expanding, as the EU will join its Executive Board for political and commercial reasons.[46] Russia missed an opportunity to become involved in this programme because it sought a leading role, despite its lack of financial resources.[47] Minatom's subsequent dealings with KEDO have focused on providing site-survey information relevant to the planned location of power reactors at Shinpo on North Korea's eastern coast based on earlier plans to build Soviet-designed power reactors there. However, even if an agreement is reached, it would provide Minatom with only a relatively small, one-time source of revenue. Instead, Minatom should be encouraged to provide fuel services for the programme with particular emphasis on storing and reprocessing the spent fuel that will come from the planned LWRs. In addition, Russia could play a useful role in receiving and eventually reprocessing the spent fuel rods unloaded from North Korea's controversial 5 megawatt reactor. The resulting plutonium could be purchased by Russia or another country rather than being returned to the Korean Peninsula.

Such an arrangement would involve Minatom in an important non-proliferation effort on the Russian border. It would also supply it with a possible source of hard currency income. Thus, the US could provide Moscow with advanced payments under the HEU deal to ensure that Russia can become a paying member of KEDO, which then creates possibilities for securing contracts associated with constructing and servicing the LWRs.

Russia's commercial nuclear involvement in the Korean peninsula could also take place within the broader context of establishing an 'Asiatom' or Pacific Atomic Energy Community (PACATOM) organisation, an Asian regional fuel-cycle arrangement modelled after the European Atomic Energy Community (EURATOM), which encourages transparency in member's civilian nuclear activities.[48] The rapid growth of nuclear power in the Asia-Pacific region and the growing problem of spent-fuel disposition are increasing pressure for new regional institutions to enhance the safety situation over the long term. Russia should become involved early on with any regional non-proliferation institution. Over time, Minatom might secure a role in providing nuclear-fuel services, which could reduce undesirable pressures for building indigenous enrichment and reprocessing facilities on the Korean peninsula.[49]

A Leadership Role for Minatom?
Given the political controversies surrounding Minatom's current nuclear exports, it is difficult to conceive of Russia as a nuclear non-

proliferation leader. But assuming that the changes discussed earlier actually occur in Minatom's export behaviour and organisational attitudes, then the Russian Federation will set an example for other countries on responsible nuclear export policies.

Minatom can play an important role in promoting non-proliferation practices through active cooperation with other countries. It has a unique opportunity to assist former Soviet republics – particularly Ukraine and Kazakstan – that gained new responsibilities for former Soviet nuclear material and facilities without the control mechanisms that the Russian Federation has. In addition, any country that still possesses Soviet-designed nuclear-power stations and related nuclear facilities could probably use Minatom's advice and technical assistance to ensure that its facilities possess adequate nuclear safeguards and improved safety measures.

The Russian Federation might also be in a special position to encourage its nuclear clients, such as India, to take gradual steps to end its isolated position. This could include pressuring India to accept full-scale nuclear safeguards at all of its relevant facilities as a prerequisite for Minatom's construction of new reactors in India. Moscow is also in a good position to encourage China to adopt a more rigorous commitment to nuclear non-proliferation, particularly in its dealings with Pakistan. Yeltsin's active role in convincing Chinese leaders to accept the complete cessation of nuclear testing gives some credence to Moscow's potential influence. Of course, pursuing these long-term objectives must begin with Minatom, convincing the directors that their organisation has more to gain than to lose by foregoing questionable nuclear exports in favour of a stronger commitment to non-proliferation. As part of a broader non-proliferation strategy, international incentives and disincentives can help make this case to Russia's political and industrial élite.

Incentives can be used to strike a balance between the conflicting objectives of the former Soviet defence and nuclear industries, which are determined to break into the global market, and the interest of the international community in maintaining a strong non-proliferation regime controlling the spread of sensitive technologies and expertise. Incentive strategies are particularly relevant when political leaders and their country's industrial élites must make export decisions about the legal transfer of sensitive items to countries with questionable non-proliferation commitments.

A greater role for incentives does not supplant the traditional emphasis on policies that limit the spread of sensitive technologies and expertise. Instead, incentive strategies must complement elements in the broader non-proliferation regime that include diplomatic pressure and the implicit threat of sanctions.

Even though incentives appear better suited to encourage the former Soviet dual-use technology providers to give higher priority to non-proliferation concerns in their export decisions, the leverage stems partly from the expectation that the inducements can be replaced by more punitive measures.

Applying Non-Proliferation Incentives

As suggested by the assessments of *Yuzhnoye* and Minatom, an effective approach entails more than simply offering specific induce-ments to encourage or discourage a country's behaviour. Rather, the best strategies are those which aim to achieve both short-term changes in the export behaviour of former Soviet technology enterprises and long-term improvements in the attitudes of their industrial élites. Pursuing these ambitious objectives is essential for two reasons. First, it is important to foreclose possible problems that could arise if dual-use industries demand, or come to expect, recurring rewards for non-proliferation behaviour. This situation could lead to incentive 'inflation' as these firms or their political leaders threaten to engage in questionable export behaviour unless they receive periodic rewards for 'being good'. Encouraging managers of dual-use technology industries to follow a non-proliferation regime is one possible avenue for avoiding this problem. This requires persuading these leaders that they have a real and continuing economic stake in adhering to strong non-proliferation policies. They must also be convinced that failing to pursue export policies that are firmly based on such a foundation will undercut their long-term prospects in the international market-place.

Second, an effective non-proliferation strategy builds on its successes as an example to encourage other industries, or enterprises in different countries, to understand the commercial advantages of pursuing responsible export policies. This is likely to be a long-term process. An incentive strategy focusing on changing attitudes as well as behaviour might require five to ten years, if not more. And its ultimate success is far from guaranteed.

However, it offers a relatively low-cost/low-risk approach to encouraging more responsible export policies on the part of emerging technology providers. This works well in situations such as that with the former Soviet republics. In this case, both sides have a strong stake in continuing cooperation on the urgent problems of securing 'loose nukes' and minimising the possibility for nuclear smuggling.

Although incentives focusing on the emerging technology provider help address the supply side of the problem, some combination of incentives and disincentives should also be used to address the interests of the countries seeking these technologies and expertise.[1] As the source of the demand, they exert a negative influence on the struggling former Soviet defence and nuclear industries.

Potential for Change?

The notion of changing the attitudes of executives and key subgroups in the former Soviet defence and nuclear industries to greater commitment to non-proliferation standards might seem optimistic given the current difficult economic conditions. However, the historical examples of Argentina, Brazil and South Africa give credence to the idea that, under the right conditions, countries can make fundamental shifts in their commitments.[2] These countries evolved from a proliferation problem to active supporters of robust non-proliferation policies. Not only have they set examples to be followed, they have also assumed various leadership roles. South Africa played a leading part in the complex negotiations surrounding the NPT Review and Extension conference; Argentina chaired the NSG and Brazil has become a strong proponent of the MTCR. Although far less important than internal dynamics in bringing about these basic changes in security perspectives, external incentives did play a significant reinforcing role by encouraging and supporting internal factions.[3] In addition, continuing incentive strategies might be desirable to counteract the possibility of retreat. This appears to account for the US decision to remove long-standing restrictions on civil nuclear exports to Argentina on the grounds that it now has an 'exemplary recent non-proliferation record'.[4] Thus, while internal considerations largely account for such basic policy transformations, external incentives can play an important role as well.

incentives need time to succeed

Sustaining Incentives

Incentives need time to succeed because industrial élites will not change their attitudes rapidly. Sustaining an effective incentive strategy is complicated by the inevitable linkage of various policy and political issues. In some cases, *policy linkage* can have a positive effect in promoting a non-proliferation agenda. For example, the economic benefits and prestige that the Russian Space Agency achieved after Moscow's changed its export policy following the *Glavkosmos*–ISRO dispute with Washington is tangible evidence of the benefits that can result. An incentive strategy should also seek to take advantage of opportunities for policy linkage by using the positive experience of one emerging technology provider to influence other national and industry decision-makers. More often, however, policy-makers must deal with the negative aspects of linkage by making trade-offs between competing foreign-policy objectives. A good example is Washington's concern that altering its MTCR entry policy to accommodate Ukraine could set an undesirable precedent and create problems with members who have already accepted these demanding conditions.

An added challenge to sustaining an incentive strategy arises from the possibility of *political linkage* between seemingly disparate policy issues. If strongly negative, this linkage can undermine domestic political support for international incentive strategies. This form of negative cross-linkage can arise if powerful domestic groups in either country have interests that are detrimentally affected by the proposed incentive strategy. For example, Washington's leeway in offering Russia and Ukraine access to the US commercial satellite space-launch market has been constrained by concern for domestic space manufacturers and their supporters on Capitol Hill.

Implications for Non-Proliferation Policies

As the two cases addressed in this paper illustrate, non-proliferation incentive strategies must be tailored to specific circumstances. However, the problems of dealing with Ukraine's aerospace industry and Russia's Minatom pose similar challenges to the inter-national community. Policy-makers have to encourage emerging technology providers to adhere not only to the letter of their country's non-proliferation obligations, but also to the general spirit of the regime. International incentives can play an essential role by encouraging these economically desperate industries to be more self-restrained in exporting sensitive dual-use technologies and expertise. Although international incentives relevant to both Ukraine's aerospace industries and Russia's Minatom have been offered by the US and other international supporters, persistent policy disagreements threaten to stall any real progress. Without prompt efforts to overcome these political hurdles, the risk that sensitive technologies and know-how will fall into the hands of proliferators, either through deliberate exports or inadvertent actions on the part of these emerging technology providers, is likely to grow.

Non-proliferation incentive strategies are not a panacea for every worrisome case of sensitive dual-use technology exports. However, political and economic inducements have a special role to play in dealing with the emerging technology providers that are a legacy of the former Soviet defence industry. Carefully designed international incentives can help transform these struggling former dual-use technology enterprises from potentially troublesome sources of sensitive technologies to enterprises that exhibit responsible export behaviour.

notes

Acknowledgements

The author would like to acknowledge the support of Rose Gottemoeller in producing this study, as well as the assistance of Amy Truesdell.

Chapter 1

[1] For example, see William C. Potter (ed.), *International Nuclear Trade and Nonproliferation: The Challenge of the Emerging Suppliers* (Lexington, MA: Lexington Books, 1990); Potter and Harlan W. Jencks (eds), *The International Missile Bazaar: The New Suppliers' Network* (Boulder, CO: Westview Press, 1994); and Leonard S. Spector with Jacqueline R. Smith, *Nuclear Ambitions: The Spread of Nuclear Weapons 1989–1990* (Boulder, CO: Westview Press, 1990), particularly pp. 29–48.

[2] Nicolay Novichkov, 'Russian Space Chief Voices Dire Warnings', *Aviation Week and Space Technology*, vol. 146, no. 1, 6 January 1997, p. 26.

[3] See Kevin P. O'Prey, *A Farewell to Arms?: Russia's Struggles with Defence Conversion* (New York: Twentieth Century Fund Press, 1995), especially Chapter 4.

[4] *Ibid.*, pp. 20–21.

[5] Julian Cooper, 'The Soviet Union and the Successor Republics: Defence Industries Coming to Terms with Disunion', in Herbert Wulf (ed.), *Arms Industry Limited* (Oxford: Oxford University Press for the Stockholm International Peace Research Institute, 1993), pp. 87–108.

[6] Elina Kirchenko, 'Russia's Export Control System: The Mechanism of Executive Branch Cooperation', *The Monitor: Nonproliferation, Demilitarization and Arms Control* (Athens: GA, University of Georgia, Center for International Trade and Security), vol. 1, no. 2, Spring 1995, pp. 1, 21; and D. L. Averre, 'Proliferation, Export Controls and Russian National Security', *Contemporary Security*

Policy, vol. 17, no. 2, August 1996, pp. 185–226.

[7] Leonard S. Spector and Mark G. McDonough with Evan S. Medeiros, *Tracking Nuclear Proliferation* (Washington DC: Carnegie Endowment for International Peace, 1995), pp. 177–87; and Lewis A. Dunn, *Containing Nuclear Proliferation* Adelphi Paper 263 (London: Brassey's for the IISS, 1991), pp. 28–34.

[8] Peter A. Clausen, 'US Nuclear Exports and the Non-Proliferation Regime', in Jed C. Snyder and Samuel F. Wells, Jr (eds), *Limiting Nuclear Proliferation* (Cambridge, MA: Ballinger Publishing Company, 1985), p. 195.

[9] *Ibid.*; and Gary Clyde Hufbauer, Jeffrey J. Schott and Kimberly Ann Elliott, *Economic Sanctions Reconsidered: Supplemental Case Histories* (Washington DC: Institute for International Economics, 1990), pp. 354, 378–85.

[10] Thomas W. Lippman and Paul Blustein, 'No Stiff US Sanctions on China and Pakistan', *Washington Post*, 18 April 1996; and Zachary S. Davis, 'China's Nonproliferation and Export Control Policies', *Asian Survey*, vol. 35, no. 6, June 1995, pp. 587–603.

[11] John Bray, 'Sanctions: Sticks to Beat Rogue States', *The World Today*, vol. 52, no. 8–9, August/September 1996, pp. 206–8.

[12] See the forthcoming study from the Carnegie Endowment for International Peace, Washington DC, tentatively entitled, *The Soviet-Russia Sale of Cryogenic Booster Technology to India and US Enforcement of the Missile Technology Control Regime.*

[13] 'Trilateral Statement by the Presidents of the US, Russia and Ukraine', *US Department of State Dispatch Supplement* (Washington DC: US Government Printing Office, January 1994), pp. 19–20.

[14] William C. Potter, *The Politics of Nuclear Renunciation: The Case of Belarus, Kazakstan and Ukraine* (Washington DC: Henry L. Stimson Center, April 1995), especially pp. 42–50; and Sherman W. Garnett, 'The Sources and Conduct of Ukrainian Nuclear Policy: November 1992 to January 1994', in George Quester (ed.), *The Nuclear Challenge in Russia and the New States of Eurasia* (Armonk, NY: M. E. Sharpe, 1995), pp. 125–51.

[15] See Jessica E. Stern, 'US Assistance Programs for Improving MPC&A in the Former Soviet Union', *The Nonproliferation Review*, vol. 3, no. 2, Winter 1996, and Jason Ellis 'Nunn-Lugar's Mid-Life Crisis', *Survival*, vol 39, no. 1, Spring 1997, pp. 84–110.

[16] Glenn E. Schweitzer, *Moscow DMZ: The Story of the International Effort to Convert Russian Weapons Science to Peaceful Purposes* (Armonk, NY: M. E. Sharpe, 1996).

[17] Rose Gottemoeller, 'The Proliferation Threat of Weapons of Mass Destructions and US Security Interests', unpublished paper prepared for the Aspen Strategy Group Meeting, Aspen, CO, August 1996.

Chapter 2

[1] Debra D. Facktor and Robert J. Blons, *Space Activities in Ukraine* (Arlington, VA: ANSER Center for International Aerospace Cooperation, September 1996), p. 11.

[2] Daniel H. Van Hulle, *Moscow*

Office Report No. 94 (Arlington, VA: ANSER Center for International Aerospace Cooperation, August 1994), p. 94–2 .

[3] Matthew Brzezinski, 'Here Success Is Spelled "Dnepropetrovsk"', *Wall Street Journal*, 28 January 1997.

[4] R. Jeffrey Smith, 'Iraq Buying Missile Parts Covertly', *Washington Post*, 16 October 1995.

[5] Bill Gertz, 'Kiev Imperils US Aid with Libya Arms Deal', *Washington Times*, 9 December 1996. Ukraine is estimated to have inherited some 132 *Scud* missiles and 140 FROG or SS-21 shorter-range ballistic-missile systems from the break-up of the Soviet Union. See *The Military Balance, 1996/97* (Oxford: Oxford University Press for the IISS, 1996), p. 101.

[6] R. Jeffrey Smith, 'Ukraine Agrees to Follow Missile Control Treaty', *Washington Post*, 14 May 1994.

[7] Alan George, 'Ukraine Slows Libyan Missile Progress', *Flight International*, vol. 144, 21 July 1993.

[8] Yanina Sokolovskaya, 'No Need to Focus Search for Chinese Spies Away from Dnipropetrovsk', *Izvestiya*, FBIS-SOV-96-036, 22 February 1996, pp. 14–15.

[9] Brian Knowlton, 'US Warns Russians on SS-18 Sales to Chinese', *International Herald Tribune*, 22 May 1996, p. 1; and Evan S. Medeiros, 'US Warns Russia, Ukraine on Missile-Related Sales to China', *Arms Control Today*, vol. 26, no. 4, May/June 1996, p. 24.

[10] John C. Baker, 'Non-Proliferation Incentives Project: Aerospace Industries Workshop and Ukraine Trip Report', IISS, London, August 1996, p. 12.

[11] James Hackett, 'Trail of Missile Potential', *Washington Times*, 10 December 1996.

[12] Yevgeni Sharov, 'Ukraine and the MTCR', *The Monitor*, vol. 1, no. 2, Spring 1995, pp. 21–22; and Richard H. Speier, 'The Missile Technology Control Regime', in Trevor Findlay (ed.), *Chemical Weapons and Missile Proliferation* (Boulder, CO: Lynne Rienner Publishers, 1991), pp. 115–21.

[13] Gary Bertsch and Victor Zaborsky, 'Missile Proliferation and US and Ukrainian Interests', paper presented to the International Security Studies Section of the International Studies Association, Atlanta, Georgia, 2 November 1996.

[14] Victor Zaborsky, 'US, Ukraine Face Missile Impasse', *Defense News*, vol. 11, no. 28, 15 July 1996, p. 25.

[15] Factor and Blons, *Space Activities in Ukraine*, pp. 32–35; and 'Ukrainian–Chinese Outer Space Cooperation', 4 December 1995, *Interfax* News Service, FBIS-SOV-95-233, 5 December 1995, pp. 55–56.

[16] Factor and Blons, *Space Activities in Ukraine*, p. 35.

[17] Warren Ferster, 'Russia Drops Plans for Ukraine's *Zenit*', *Space News*, vol. 7, no. 19, 13 May 1996, p. 1.

[18] 'Ukraine: Prospects for Implementing Space Launch Programme Viewed', *Uryadovyy Kuryer*, FBIS-SOV-96-045, 6 March 1996, p. 48; and Van Hulle, *Moscow Office Report No. 94*, p. 2.

[19] Jospeh C. Anselmo, 'Iridium Marks Dawn Of New Industry', *Aviation Week and Space Technology*, vol. 146, no. 2, 13 January 1997, p. 363.

[20] Paul Proctor, 'Sea Launch Venture Eyes Mid-1988 First

Flight', *Aviation Week and Space Technology*, vol. 145, no. 5, 29 July 1996, pp. 56–59; Scott Lafee, 'Sea Launch Is Go', *New Scientist*, vol. 152, no. 2052, 19 October 1996, pp. 36–39; and Facktor and Blons, *Space Activities in Ukraine*, p. 34.
[21] Warren Ferster, 'EarthWatch's EarlyBird Will Launch on Start-1', *Space News*, vol. 8, no. 2, 13 January 1997, pp. 1, 16.
[22] Marco Antonio Caceres, 'Satcoms Growth On Upswing', *Aviation Week and Space Technology*, vol. 146, no. 2, 13 January 1997, pp. 117–20; Peter B. de Selding, 'Launch Demand to Double, Then Drop', *Space News*, vol. 7, no. 47, 9 December 1996, pp. 4, 50; and Victor L. Zaborsky, 'Ukraine's Niche in the US Launch Market: Will Kiev's Hopes Come True?', *World Affairs*, vol. 159, no. 2, Autumn 1996, pp. 55–63.
[23] *Agreement Between the Government of the United States of America and the Government of Ukraine regarding International Trade in Commercial Space Launch Services*, (Washington DC: Office of the Press Secretary, The White House, 21 February 1996).
[24] Interview with Anatoliy M. Bulochnikov, Director, Centre on Export Controls, Moscow, 6 February 1996.
[25] US Department of Defense, *Report to Congress on Results of Foreign Launch System Comparison Study* (Washington DC: Department of Defense, 1994), pp. 9–10.
[26] See Facktor and Blons, *Space Activities in Ukraine*; and Roman Krawec, 'Ukrainian Space Policy: Contributing to National Economic Development', *Space Policy*, vol. 11, no. 2, May 1995, pp. 110–12.
[27] Bertsch and Zaborsky, 'Missile Proliferation and US and Ukrainian Interests'.
[28] The International Space Station is a multinational effort to create a continuously manned space station to support scientific and experimental work. Modular construction in orbit is planned to start in late 1999.
[29] Patrick Seitz, 'Brazilians Want Role on Space Station', *Space News*, vol. 7, no. 19, 13 May 1996, p. 3.

Chapter 3

[1] Steven Zaloga, 'The CIS Nuclear Weapons Industry', *Jane's Intelligence Review*, vol. 4, no. 9, September 1992, p. 38.
[2] Graham T. Allison, Owen R. Cote, Jr, Richard A. Falkenrath and Steven E. Miller, *Avoiding Nuclear Anarchy: Containing the Threat of Loose Russian Nuclear Weapons and Fissile Material* (Cambridge, MA: MIT Press, 1996), pp. 21, 178.
[3] *Nuclear Energy Safety Challenges in the Former Soviet Union* (Washington DC: Center for Strategic and International Studies, 1995), pp. 27–28.
[4] Robert E. Ebel, *Energy Choices in Russia* (Washington DC: Center for Strategic and International Studies, 1994), pp. 71–74.
[5] Michael Specter, 'Occupation of a Nuclear Plant Signals Russian Labor's Anger', *New York Times*, 7 December 1996.
[6] Mark Hibbs, 'Lack of Priorities Said to Mark Mikhailov-Managed Empire', *Nucleonics Week*, vol. 36, no. 50, 14 December 1995, pp. 10–11.
[7] Thomas A. Cochran, Robert S.

Norris and Oleg A. Bukharin, *Making the Russian Bomb: From Stalin to Yeltsin* (Boulder, CO: Westview Press, 1995), especially pp. 31–70; and Owen R. Cote, Jr, 'The Russian Nuclear Archipelago', in Allison , et. al., *Avoiding Nuclear Anarchy*, pp. 177–202.

[8] David Hoffman, 'Russian Turmoil Reaches Nuclear Sanctum', *Washington Post*, 22 December 1996; and International Energy Agency, *Energy Policies of the Russian Federation: 1995 Survey* (Paris: Organisation for Economic Cooperation and Development, 1995), p. 241.

[9] Stern, 'US Assistance Programs for Improving MPC&A in the Former Soviet Union', p. 29.

[10] 'Yeltsin Approves Composition of Security Council', Itar-TASS, BBC Summary of World Broadcasts, 2 August 1996, p. B/1.

[11] Ghermar Lomanov, 'Deadly Raw Material Can be Converted into Russia's National Asset', *Moscow News*, 4 April 1993; and Matthew L. Wald and Michael R. Gordon, 'Russia Treasures Plutonium, But US Wants to Destroy It', *New York Times*, 19 August 1994.

[12] John P. Holdren, John F. Ahearne, Richard L. Garwin, Wolfgang K. H. Panofsky and Matthew Bunn, 'Excess Weapons Plutonium: How to Reduce a Clear and Present Danger', *Arms Control Today*, vol. 26, no. 9, 26 November/December 1996, pp. 3–9, and the official study by the US–Russian Plutonium Disposition Steering Committee, *Joint United States–Russian Plutonium Disposition Study* (Washington DC: Office of Fissile Materials Disposition, US Department of Energy, September 1996).

[13] Ann MacLachlan, 'G-7 Experts Favor Both Burning and Vitrifying Weapons Pu', *Nucleonics Week*, vol. 37, no. 49, 5 December 1996, pp. 13–14.

[14] 'Nuclear Energy Committee to Expand Foreign Cooperation', Interfax, FBIS-SOV-95-215, 7 November 1995, p. 15.

[15] 'Nuclear Ministry's Exports Reach 1.65bn Dollars in 1995', Interfax, SWB/SUW/0417 WA/7, 12 January 1996, p. WA/7.

[16] The Uranium Institute, *Nuclear Fuel and Free Trade* (London: Uranium Institute, September 1995), p. 19.

[17] Jonathan Benjamin-Alvarado, 'Cuban Nuclear Developments', *The Monitor*, vol. 2, nos. 1–2, Winter–Spring 1996, pp. 1, 5–7.

[18] Allison, *et. al., Avoiding Nuclear Anarchy*, p. 34.

[19] William C. Potter, 'Before the Deluge?: Assessing the Threat of Nuclear Leakage From the Post-Soviet States', *Arms Control Today*, vol. 25, no. 8, October 1995, pp. 9–16; and Oleg Bukharin, 'Nuclear Safeguards and Security in the Former Soviet Union', *Survival*, vol. 36, no. 4, Winter 1994–95, pp. 53–72.

[20] 'Nuclear Security After the Moscow Summit', IISS, *Strategic Comments*, vol. 2, no. 5 , June 1996; and Vladimir A. Orlov, 'The Moscow Nuclear Summit and the Status of Russia's Smuggling Threat', *The Nonproliferation Review*, vol. 3, no. 3, Spring–Summer 1996, pp. 80–85.

[21] David A. Kay, 'Denial and Deception Practices of WMD Proliferators: Iraq and Beyond', *Washington Quarterly*, vol. 18, no. 1, Winter 1995, pp. 85–105.

[22] Steven Greenhouse, 'US Warns

Russia Again on Iran Deal', *New York Times*, 9 April 1995.
[23] Evan S. Medeiros, 'Russian–Iranian Reactor Contract Restarts Work at Bushehr Complex', *Arms Control Today*, vol. 26, no. 4, May/June 1996, p. 25.
[24] David A. Schwarzbach, *Iran's Nuclear Program: Energy or Weapons?* (Washington DC: Natural Resources Defense Council, 1995), pp. 13–22; and David Albright, 'An Iranian Bomb?', *The Bulletin of the Atomic Scientists*, vol. 51, no. 4, July/August 1995, p. 22; and US Senate Foreign Relations Committee Hearing: *US Policy Toward Iran and Iraq*, 104th Congress, 1st session. (Washington DC: US Government Printing Office, 1995), pp. 21–25, 31–32.
[25] Albright, 'An Iranian Bomb?', p. 22; and Averre, 'Proliferation, Export Controls and Russian National Security', pp. 203–5.
[26] Michael R. Gordon, 'Russia Selling Atomic Plants to India; US Protests Deal', *New York Times*, 6 February 1997.
[27] Schwarzbach, *Iran's Nuclear Program*, pp. 6, 10–12; and Nick Rufford, 'China Defies US with Iran Nuclear Deal', *Sunday Times*, 15 October 1995.
[28] The Monterey Institute for International Studies and the Carnegie Endowment for International Peace, *Nuclear Successor States of the Soviet Union* (Monterey, CA: MIIS/CEIP, May 1996), pp. 66–68.
[29] Gary Bertsch and Igor Khripunov, 'Privatization Carries Cost: Russian Firms Shrug at Proliferation Concerns', *The Monitor*, vol. 2, no. 4, Autumn 1996, pp. 17–18.
[30] *Proliferation and Export Controls* (London: Deltac Limited and Saferworld, 1995), pp. 15–19; and Spector, *Tracking Nuclear Proliferation*, pp. 179–83.
[31] Energy Information Administration, 'Uncertainties in the US Uranium Market', *World Nuclear Outlook* (Washington DC: US Department of Energy, 1995), p. 128.
[32] Crag Cerniello, 'US, Russia Amend HEU Deal, Accelerating Implementation Pace', *Arms Control Today*, vol. 26, no. 9, November/December 1996, p. 16.
[33] Stern, 'US Assistance Programs', p. 26; Oleg Bukharin and William Potter, 'Potatoes Were Guarded Better', *The Bulletin of Atomic Scientists*, vol. 51, no. 3, May/June 1995, pp. 46–50.
[34] Stern, 'US Assistance Programs, p. 26.
[35] *Ibid.*, pp. 25–30; and Allison, *et. al.*, Avoiding Nuclear Anarchy, pp. 83–88.
[36] US General Accounting Office, *Nuclear Safety: International Assistance Efforts to Make Soviet-Designed Reactors Safer* (Washington DC: GAO, 1994), pp. 3–11, 28–31.
[37] International Atomic Energy Agency, *International Assistance to Upgrade the Safety of Soviet-designed Nuclear Power Plants* (Vienna: IAEA, 1993), pp. 21–31.
[38] 'France, Germany, Russia Agree on MOX Demo to Burn Weapons Grade Plutonium', *Post-Soviet Nuclear & Defense Monitor* (Washington DC: Exchange/Monitor Publications, vol. 3, no. 26, 8 November 1996), p. 9.
[39] See Allison, *et. al.*, *Avoiding Nuclear Anarchy*, Appendix C, pp. 229–92.

40 Mark Hibbs, 'Russia–Iran Bushehr PWR Project Shows Little Concrete Progress', *Nucleonics Week*, vol. 52, no. 3, 26 September 1996, pp. 3–4.
41 'Russia, Iran, China and India to Jointly Develop Nuclear Reactor', Open Media Research Institute (OMRI), *Daily Digest, Russia*, 1 March 1996.
42 Baker, 'Ukraine Trip Report', pp. 5, 12.
43 Interview by Andrei Kolesnikov with Yevgeny Reshetnikov, Deputy Minister of the Russian Federation's Atomic Industry, 'Russia Is Losing the Atomic War', *Moscow News*, 17 June 1994.
44 Colin Woodard, 'Fighting for the Scraps', *Bulletin of the Atomic Scientists*, vol. 52, no. 3, May/June 1996, pp. 56–59.
45 Korean Peninsula Energy Development Organisation, *Annual Report 1995* (New York: KEDO, 1995); and 'The US–North Korea Nuclear Accord: Prospects', IISS, *Strategic Comments*, vol. 1, no. 2, 22 February 1995.
46 Kathleen Hart, 'European Union Finalizing Terms to Join KEDO as Board Member', *Nucleonics Week* vol. 38, no. 3, 16 January 1997, p. 16.
47 Valery I. Denisov, 'The US–DPRK Nuclear Deal: A Russian Perspective', *Nonproliferation Review*, vol. 3, no. 3, Spring–Summer 1996, pp. 74–79.
48 'Nuclear Energy Boom in Asia-Pacific Sparks Proposals for an "Asiatom"', *Nuclear Fuel* vol. 21, no. 24, 18 November 1996.
49 Robert A. Manning, 'PACATOM: Nuclear Cooperation in Asia', *Washington Quarterly*, vol. 20, no. 2, Spring 1997, pp. 217–32;

and Michael J. Mazarr, *North Korea and the Bomb: A Case Study in Nonproliferation* (London: Macmillan Press, 1995), pp. 68–69, 118–20.

Conclusion

1 Virginia I. Foran and Leonard S. Spector, 'The Application of Incentives to Nuclear Non-Proliferation', in David Cortright (ed.), *The Price of Peace: Incentives and International Conflict Prevention* (Lanhan, MD: Rowman and Littlefield, forthcoming, 1997); and William J. Long, 'Trade and Technology Incentives and Bilateral Cooperation', *International Studies Quarterly*, vol. 40, no. 1, March 1996, pp. 77–106.
2 Mitchell Reiss, *Bridled Ambition: Why Countries Constrain Their Nuclear Capabilities* (Washington DC: The Woodrow Wilson Press, 1995), pp. 7–88; and Waldo Stumpf, 'South Africa's Nuclear Weapons Program: From Deterrence to Dismantlement', *Arms Control Today*, vol. 25, no. 8, December 1995/January 1996, pp. 3–8; Wyn Bowen and Andrew Koch, 'Non-Proliferation is Embraced by Brazil', *Jane's Intelligence Review*, vol. 8, no. 6, June 1996, pp. 283–87.
3 John R. Redick, Julio C. Carasales, and Paulo S. Wrobel, 'Nuclear Rapprochement: Argentina, Brazil and the Nonproliferation Regime', *Washington Quarterly*, vol. 18, no. 1, Winter 1995, p. 119.
4 'US Lifts Export Restrictions Against Argentina', *Nuclear Proliferation News*, no. 3, 8 September 1995, p. 20.

For Product Safety Concerns and Information please contact our EU
representative GPSR@taylorandfrancis.com
Taylor & Francis Verlag GmbH, Kaufingerstraße 24, 80331 München, Germany

www.ingramcontent.com/pod-product-compliance
Ingram Content Group UK Ltd.
Pitfield, Milton Keynes, MK11 3LW, UK
UKHW021437080625
459435UK00011B/286